SWINDON TOWN
Miscellany

SWINDON TOWN
Miscellany

Robins Trivia,
History, Facts & Stats

ANDREW HAWES

SWINDON TOWN
Miscellany

All statistics, facts and figures are correct as of 1st August 2009

© Andrew Hawes

Andrew Hawes has asserted his rights in accordance with the Copyright, Designs
and Patents Act 1988 to be identified as the author of this work.

Published By:
Pitch Publishing (Brighton) Ltd
A2 Yeoman Gate
Yeoman Way
Durrington
BN13 3QZ

Email: info@pitchpublishing.co.uk
Web: www.pitchpublishing.co.uk

First published 2009

A catalogue record for this book is available from the British Library.

10-digit ISBN: 1-9054115-8-8
13-digit ISBN: 978-1-9054115-8-0

Printed and bound in Malta by Gutenburg Press

To Helen, for just being there – especially
the bit about David Holdsworth.

FOREWORD

Swindon Town is the perfect club to write a Miscellany about.

I'm sure fans of teams throughout the country have stories to tell, but even though I've only covered the club for just eight of their 125 plus years, I've already had enough first-hand experience to know that the County Ground is always an interesting place to be.

In that time I've seen everything from the club being hours from extinction, through managers conducting interviews in their pyjamas, to Swindon's greatest single-season goalscorer since World War II. There is always something happening, good and bad, and frankly sometimes it's difficult to keep up.

That's where books like this come in so useful. Reading it, there were more than a few smiles about things I have seen at the club – but had forgotten about – and plenty completely new to me. Most football books tend to be either one thing or another. You get statistics, funny stories or insights into the running of a club, but not often in the same few pages.

In what other book would you find a list of Swindon's greatest goalscorers and a tale of the goalkeeper happily chatting away to fans while the Town were on the attack? Even the most diehard fans will find something new, interesting or just plain bizarre in these pages.

And, with it being Swindon, there's plenty of the bizarre. Obviously.

Ed Hadwin,
BBC Wiltshire

ACKNOWLEDGEMENTS

There are several useful sources I have consulted while putting this together, but none is better than the fantastic http://www.swindon-town-fc.co.uk website. It's a must-visit and is a wonderful online chronicle. Naturally Dick Mattick's history of the club has proved invaluable, as has Peter Matthews' excellent book *John Trollope Record Breaker*, and his biography of Don Rogers.

I thank Peter for permission to re-tell a tale, while Lou Macari's autobiography also made a fascinating read. The staff at Swindon library also deserve thanks for putting up with me sending microfilm spinning off in all directions on several occasions when consulting the *Evening Advertiser* back issues.

INTRODUCTION

My first visit to Swindon Town is a very vague memory. I can recall my dad taking me – the main stand appearing vast – and two Fulham fans sitting in front of us. Swindon went on to lose 4-3. I couldn't name you a single player, the year or what happened, other than the score for several years, until I started writing this book. Apparently it was in August 1980, making me 7 at the time and I saw David Peach make a positive contribution, which I gather was pretty rare.

It's been both fun and challenging to put this together and I hope it makes for entertaining reading. I think the most demanding thing in some ways is digging into the rise of the club of the 1980s and the illegal payments affair which accompanied it.

There are plenty of thanks to be handed out. I'd like to thank the people at Pitch for asking me to do this and their support for a first time author; plus note the help of Ed Hadwin of BBC Radio Swindon, the club's Chris Tanner, Town fans Steve Kaczmar, Paul Davis, Paul Wardell and David Mouland, author Peter Matthews, Aldershot's Graham Brookland and especially Sussex journalist Andy Arlidge for many anecdotes of yore. Together we formed a much needed red corner of the Brighton & Hove Albion press box for some time. Chris Scott also deserves a mention for being such a friendly host on any professional visit to the County Ground for a match.

After completing this book I think I have even more enthusiasm and interest in the club than before. That would be a grand ambition for me to pass on so I just hope what follows makes the reader raise an eyebrow and go "really?" or at least bring back some good memories.

Andrew Hawes, 2009

OVER TALKATIVE TANNOY MAN

Swindon tannoy announcer Peter Lewis was abruptly sacked midway through a game in 1995. Swindon were playing Bolton Wanderers when then player-manager Steve McMahon was given a red card in the first half by referee Graham Barber for a late challenge. Lewis came on the tannoy at half-time to say; "I've seen some crap refereeing decisions in my time, but..." with the rest drowned out by the crowd's hilarity. He ended up being escorted from the ground by the club secretary. Just to add to a rotten evening for Lewis, Swindon went on to lose 1-0 to a late goal from Alan Thompson.

THE ORIGINS

It now seems to be accepted that Swindon Town's life started in 1879, though for a long time it was regarded that it was in 1881 when the 'Swindon Football Club' came into existence. In that year a merger was agreed between the Spartans of Old Swindon and St. Mark's Young Mens' Friendly Society following a match between the two teams. Reverend William Pitt was the Spartans' captain and is seen as the father of the club. Further research, conducted by Swindon historian Paul Plowman, found the Reverend Pitt talking of forming the club in 1879 at a speech in 1911 to mark the club's Southern League title triumph. The Reverend Pitt appears to have begun a Swindon AFC in 1879, which became the Spartans before the merger with the Friendly Society. The 1879 origin is now accepted by the club, which has it as the formation date on the current crest.

DOING THE BUSINESS ON DERBY DAY

Swindon have one of the best home records in any local derby when it comes to playing Oxford United. Town's rivals recorded just one win at the County Ground in 24 games during their stay in the Football League. That was in February 1973. Swindon's biggest home win in the fixture, a 4-0 victory, came in 1972 with Arthur Horsfield hitting a hat-trick. Swindon also beat Oxford 4-1 at home in consecutive seasons in 1997 and 1998 and the last derby game at the County Ground (for now) was in October 2000. Alan Reeves and Giuliano Grazioli scored in a 2-1 win.

PENALTY KINGS

Here are Swindon's leading ten scorers from the penalty spot:

Billy Tout 42
Don Rogers..24
Wally Dickenson 19
Paul Bodin 17
Ernie Hunt 17
Ray McHale 14
Jack Johnson..11
David Moss...11
Trevor Anderson..10
Paul Rideout 10

PUTTING ONE OVER THE WORLD CUP WINNERS

One of Swindon's best ever FA Cup results came against West Ham United in the 1966/67 season. Swindon, then in Division Three, held the Hammers to a 3-3 draw at Upton Park. Predictably, Geoff Hurst opened the scoring, but Don Rogers replied almost immediately after a one-two with Willie Penman. Hurst's second was cancelled out by Dennis Brown then Don Rogers scored to make it 3-2 to Swindon with nineteen minutes remaining. In true World Cup style, Hurst completed his hat-trick six minutes later, which meant a replay. Around two thousand fans were locked out of the County Ground for the game but a crowd of just under 26,000 did make it inside to see the Hammers beaten. Willie Penman's first-half goal meant Swindon were in front with 12 minutes to go before the Hammers drew level via John Sissons. But, the Third Division side finished the stronger. Two notable figures combined to make it 2-1 as Don Rogers calmly controlled and swept home John Trollope's cross. Then industrious forward Ken Skeen made the win certain with a goal in the last minute of normal time. There was no resting of senior players by West Ham; World Cup-winning trio Bobby Moore, Geoff Hurst and Martin Peters played in both games. Swindon went on to reach the fifth round and were only knocked out by Nottingham Forest after a second replay.

SWEET SUCCESS AT ASHTON GATE

Swindon have had the rare pleasure of beating both Bristol City and Bristol Rovers at Ashton Gate. Lou Macari's side met Rovers at Bristol City's ground on April 11th 1987. It was Rovers' first season in exile in Bath and the game was moved back to Bristol from Twerton Park to try and raise funds, with the Gas struggling both on and off the pitch. Town trailed in a memorable local derby 3-2, but a brilliant individual goal from Dave Bamber – he turned and shot from the edge of the area – made it 3-3. A minute later a Jimmy Quinn volley gave Swindon a 4-3 victory on their way to the play-offs.

CUP FINAL KEY TO THE FUTURE

The 1987 FA Cup final classic between Coventry and Spurs featured no less than five different players who would go on to play for Swindon. Central defender Brian Kilcline and winger Dave Bennett helped Coventry lift the Cup in a 3-2 win. John Gorman signed Kilcline for Swindon in the Premier League, while Bennett had a spell at the County Ground marred by injury. In the beaten Spurs side there were two future Town managers, Glenn Hoddle and Ossie Ardiles, plus Paul Allen, who was part of Steve McMahon's Division Two title-winning squad.

WHAT OFF SEASON?

Two of Swindon's Southern League side of 1919/20 were chosen to take part in an FA tour of South Africa, thus effectively being part of an unofficial international team. Bertie Davies and Dave Rogers were two attack-minded players. The pair set off by boat from Southampton straight after the season ended and they didn't return to England until the start of August.

CIVIC DUTY

The County Ground offers conference and hospitality facilities but once a year or so it also performs an important civic role – as a polling station. One of the bars inside the North Stand was converted for use in the 2009 council and European elections for voters to do their thing.

MEET THE MANAGERS

This is a list of Swindon managers from 1900 to the present day, excluding the caretakers. Sam Allen was effectively manager/secretary in the early days. The gap in the 1955/56 season is due to a club committee picking the team, assisted for a time by a player-coach Geoff Fox.

Sam Allen	1902/33
Ted Vizard	1933/39
Neil Harris	1939/41
Louis Page	1945/53
Maurice Lindley	1953/55
Bert Head	1956/65
Danny Williams	1965/69
Fred Ford	1969/71
Dave Mackay	1971/72
Les Allen	1972/74
Danny Williams	1974/78
Bobby Smith	1978/80
John Trollope	1980/83
Ken Beamish	1983/84
Lou Macari	1984/89
Ossie Ardiles	1989/91
Glenn Hoddle	1991/93
John Gorman	1993/94
Steve McMahon	1994/99
Jimmy Quinn	1999/2000
Colin Todd	2000
Andy King	2000/01
Roy Evans	2001
Andy King	2001/06
Iffy Onuora	2006
Dennis Wise	2006
Paul Sturrock	2006/07
Maurice Malpas	2008
Danny Wilson	2008 to present

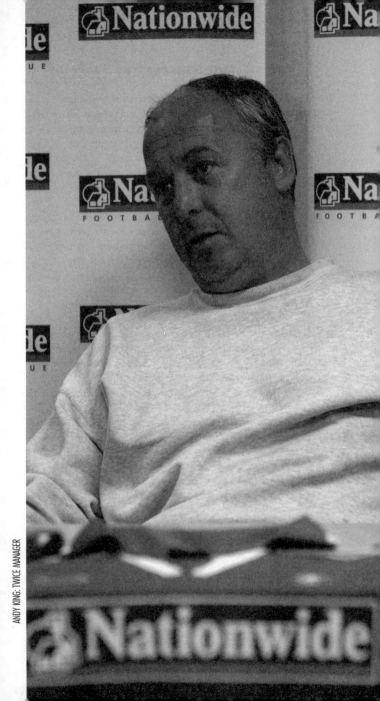

LOVING THE LEAGUE CUP: PART ONE – 1968/69

The 1969 League Cup remains Swindon's only major honour. In some ways the trophy was the culmination of Danny Williams' patient work over previous seasons and the players insist to this day they enjoy a unique bond. The actual run to the final saw some wonderful wins over top flight opposition. After early victories over Torquay United and Bradford City, Swindon had a comfortable win over Division Two Blackburn Rovers in round three, and looked the better side in two games with top flight Coventry in round four, letting a two-goal lead slip with just four minutes to go at Highfield Road before cruising through the replay. The quarter-final saw two really tough games with Brian Clough's Derby County, who were to be Second Division champions. Swindon prevailed in the replay thanks to some magnificent defending and a Don Rogers deflected goal. The semi-final saw a first leg away win at First Division Burnley, who were on a brilliant run of form at the time, but things nearly came to an end in the second leg when Burnley dominated and established a two-goal lead. John Smith's header from Don Rogers' corner kept the tie alive, and ultimately led to a third match at a neutral venue, where they survived the sickener of a last-minute equaliser to re-assert themselves in extra time and earn a Wembley date with Arsenal. The Wembley pitch was in an even worse state than now thanks to the Horse of the Year Show. Arsenal insist there was a flu bug, but manager Williams, such a believer in fitness, saw his side come to life in extra time again. The final saw perhaps the worst goal ever at Wembley in terms of quality: a glorious fiasco in the Arsenal defence and a far-from-clean shot that limped into the net from Roger Smart, before yet another late goal to test Swindon's resolve as Bobby Gould took the match to extra time. Rogers smacked home the loose ball from a corner as Swindon got stronger and stronger. Then, after one of the worst Wembley goals came one of the best. A counter-attack saw a perfect ball by Smart to Don Rogers who had kept position just inside his own half to prevent being offside. Rogers had an age to think with a huge prize at stake, but effortlessly rounded Bob Wilson to kill the contest and complete a cup run which is part of the history of the town of Swindon – not just Swindon Town Football Club. In Swindon library's research section there is a pictorial montage of local events and sitting right at the top is the League Cup winners showing off the trophy at the town hall.

1969 LEAGUE CUP FACTS AND FIGURES

Round/Scorers	*Opponents*	*Score*
First round	Torquay United (H)	2-1
Smart, Noble		
Second round	Bradford City (A)	1-1
Smart		
Second round replay	Bradford City (H)	4-3
Smith, Rogers (pen), Smart, Noble		
Third round	Blackburn Rovers (H)	1-0
Rogers		
Fourth round	Coventry City (A)	2-2
Rogers, Smart		
Fourth round replay	Coventry City (H)	3-0
Rogers, Smart, Penman		
Quarter-final	Derby County (A)	0-0
Quarter-final replay	Derby County (H)	1-0
Rogers		
Semi-final, first leg	Burnley (A)	2-1
Harland, Noble		
Semi-final, second leg	Burnley (H)	1-2
Smith		
Semi-final replay	Burnley (The Hawthorns)	3-2
Smith, Bellamy (og), Noble		
Final	Arsenal (Wembley)	3-1
Smart, Rogers (2)		

Team: Peter Downsborough, Rod Thomas, John Trollope, Joe Butler, Frank Burrows, Stan Harland, Don Heath, Roger Smart, John Smith (Willie Penman), Peter Noble, Don Rogers.

FRASER DIGBY'S MUSICAL MEMENTO

Long-serving Swindon keeper Fraser Digby has inspired a series of increasingly surreal musical tributes on Danny Baker's 6-0-6 phone-in on BBC Radio 5 Live. The idea all came from a call-in a discussion about items listeners owned that once belonged to footballers. One rang in to confess to stealing a tortoiseshell comb from Fraser Digby's washbag while he was on a tour of the County Ground. The phrase clearly struck a chord with Danny Baker, who suggested people write a song around the idea of 'Fraser Digby's Washbag'. Since then, songs based on the purloining of the comb have been set to the tunes of *Eleanor Rigby, My Old Man's a Dustman, Sweet Home Alabama* and many others. Fraser also arrived in the studio, to Danny Baker's considerable surprise, to perform a duet – of sorts – for the *Chitty Chitty Bang Bang* version.

REDUCED TO TEARS

A particularly ignominious 7-0 defeat for Swindon at Bolton Wanderers in 1997 proved too much for BBC Wiltshire Sound reporter Stuart Mac, who was unable to stop himself crying as he began to describe the goals in his post match summary – for those who could still face the grim details. He had to be taken off air. Mac told the *Bolton Evening News* afterwards: "It was very embarrassing but I couldn't stop myself. It was just all too much. It was my last away game on the radio. The Bolton fans were absolutely magnificent... after they saw what happened in the press box they patted me on the back and said 'never mind'."

WHERE GREAT MINDS COME TO GROW

Among Swindon's players in their Southern League days around the turn of the century was an inside-forward called Herbert Chapman, who was a bit of a footballing nomad. He didn't stay long. Chapman went on to become a manager, who was with Leeds City, who ended up being disbanded due to illegal payments. He moved to Huddersfield and then Arsenal, winning the Football League for both. Chapman is also regarded as a tactical innovator, while backing the ideas of floodlighting and numbered shirts way before they were fashionable.

THE CURIOUS CURSE OF GREATER MANCHESTER

Swindon fans spent years dreading the sight of the M60, after going more than a decade without a win in the Greater Manchester area in a spell in the 1980s and 1990s. After beating Wigan Athletic 3-2 at Springfield Park in the 1987 play-offs, Town made 31 trips to Manchester United, Manchester City, Bolton Wanderers, Oldham Athletic, Stockport County, Bury and Wigan without recording a victory. Oldham's Boundary Park was the most regular haunt, with eight visits seeing three draws and five defeats. The curse was most savage in the Steve McMahon era, where Town lost 5-1 at Oldham, 6-0 at Manchester City and 7-0 at Bolton in the space of seven months. The jinx was finally broken in the new millennium, when Swindon won 3-0 at Bury early in the 2001/02 season thanks to goals from Jo Kuffour, Keith O'Halloran and David Duke.

BOOTIFUL

The 1962/63 season was badly hit by snow and ice, with Bert Head's Swindon side only able to play one match in January. Strenuous efforts were made to make the County Ground playable for the game with Queens Park Rangers. After going through some practice matches during the week with different kinds of footwear, the Town team found that basketball boots were the ideal thing to give the players some grip in the snow. The team stayed late in the dressing rooms before kick-off to avoid Rangers following suit, while QPR went through an extensive pre-match warm-up. The result was a 5-0 thumping of the Londoners, with striker Jack Smith hitting a hat-trick. The QPR manager Alec Stock had tried to get the game called off. He was not impressed, while Bata, who made the boots, followed up their success with an advertising campaign.

FANZINE CULTURE

A number of fanzines have given their own take on Swindon matter since the 1980s. The first was *Bring the Noise!* which began in 1998. In the 1990s there was the *69'er* and *The Randy Robin*. In 2000, *The Magic Roundabout* was threatened with legal action by ex-manager Steve McMahon and Chairman Rikki Hunt following a cartoon strip. The editors offered a full page apology in the next issue.

TWO GAMES IN ONE DAY

Swindon got more than their money's worth out of striker Peter Thorne on September 25th 1996. Thorne, who was coming back from flu, played for Swindon reserves in the afternoon, putting in a full ninety minutes and scoring against Charlton Athletic's second string. With the entire squad in London, manager Steve McMahon decided to put the striker on the bench for the evening's League Cup tie at Queens Park Rangers. Swindon had a 2-1 deficit to overcome from the home leg and the tie was all-square when Thorne came on in the second half. In extra time Thorne thumped home Mark Robinson's cross to complete Swindon's comeback. Then, with his job done, Thorne was substituted to end off his second game of the day. Swindon's reward for making the third round was a tie at Manchester United.

BARE-FACED CHEEK

The Millwall manager Mick McCarthy was not impressed – unlike the rest of the County Ground – after the Lions' 3-1 League Cup quarter-final defeat by Swindon in 1995. He insisted he would "bear his backside in Burton's shop window" if striker Jan Age Fjortoft had meant to score with a truly outstanding effort from the corner of the penalty area that curled in at the last second, right at Kasey Keller's far post. This author is convinced Fjortoft did – but luckily for those out shopping in south London the McCarthy buttocks remain unseen by the general public.

PAYING THE PENALTY

On December 17th 1989, Swindon conceded three penalties in six minutes, but still beat West Bromwich Albion. Swindon were two goals up at The Hawthorns, thanks to Duncan Shearer and Steve White, before the lunacy ensued. Firstly, Colin Calderwood and Chris Whyte tangled in the area for penalty one. Bernard McNally's spot kick was tipped round the post by Fraser Digby. From the following corner, the Baggies were invited to have another go, with Shearer accused of handball. Graham Harbey sent penalty two over the bar and vaguely towards Jupiter. Four minutes after that, Don Goodman broke into the box and Jon Gittens brought him down. Goodman struck an excellent penalty into the top corner, but Town were still able to win 2-1 as the Baggies reflected on their inefficiency from 12 yards out.

COLIN CALDERWOOD

Lou Macari's eye for a player saw him bring in two in Swindon's top ten all-time appearance makers. In the summer of 1985, Swindon paid £27,500 for Colin Calderwood, a young Scottish defender who was with Mansfield Town. Macari clearly saw something both in his ability and character. The centre-back lifted the Division Four trophy at the age of 21 and was an automatic choice for Macari, Ossie Ardiles and Glenn Hoddle throughout his spell with the club, which directly coincided with the spectacular rise through the leagues. The Scot captained Swindon to four promotions in total, including 1990, completing the journey from the basement to the top flight. He also faced arrest in the tax scandal that engulfed the club but was quickly released without charge. Seemingly always calm and invaluable in organising any defence he was part of, Calderwood also chipped in with some memorable goals during his eight seasons in Wiltshire. He scored a free kick from at least 45 yards out against Port Vale and netted the winner when Swindon beat the Division One champions Newcastle United in 1993. His last game turned out to be the Wembley play-off final win over Leicester City. After leaving for Spurs in that summer to be reunited with Ossie Ardiles, Calderwood received a spontaneous round of applause and his familiar chant of "Oh Colin Colin, Colin Colin Colin Colin Calderwood" as soon as he emerged at White Hart Lane from the Swindon fans. After that came overdue recognition by Scotland, playing in Euro 96 and the 1998 World Cup. After his playing career finished Calderwood's organisational skills have been put to good use as a manager, leading Northampton Town and Nottingham Forest to promotion, while it's understood he was close to returning to Swindon as manager in December 2008 before Danny Wilson took the job.

YOU'LL NEVER HAVE IT SO GOOD

Swindon's biggest victory in the Football League was in their first ever game! Town demolished Luton 9-1 on August 28th 1920 at the County Ground with Harold Fleming scoring four of the goals. Billy Batty scored twice, with Bertie Davies and Bob Jefferson also on target. Luton were also generous enough to contribute an own goal. The two sides met in the return fixture at Luton a week later. This time Town were on the wrong end of a 2-0 defeat.

TOWN'S TIME WITH THE MATCH-FIXERS

Swindon didn't realise what they were getting when they signed the Scottish forward Jimmy Gauld from Plymouth Argyle and David 'Bronco' Layne from Rotherham United ahead of the 1959/60 season. Gauld played for just one season at the County Ground, and Swindon were thumped 6-1 at Port Vale in their penultimate fixture in Division Three, a seemingly meaningless affair with neither side having anything to play for. The *Evening Advertiser* report on the Monday described the Swindon defence as "slow and hesitant" and "rarely showing any sign of forthrightness". It appeared to be just one of those off-days when Swindon rounded off the season with a home victory over Coventry City. However, despite Swindon paying a hefty sum for him Gauld was let go after just one season in Wiltshire. He moved to St. Johnstone and his career was ended when he broke his leg at Mansfield Town. Layne, a prolific striker, left Swindon midway through the next campaign to return to his native Yorkshire, signing for Bradford City. He hit 35 goals in 46 matches but was not part of that side so badly beaten at Vale Park. In 1964, Gauld sold his story in an interview to the *Sunday People* for a reported £7,000, exposing his corrupt activities. He revealed that, in 1962, Gauld and Layne bumped into each other at a Mansfield game. Gauld talked to Layne about match-fixing and how there was easy money to be made betting on games where you knew the outcome. So, it ended up that Layne, now a Sheffield Wednesday player, suggested to teammates Peter Swan and Tony Kay that they bet on their side to lose at Ipswich Town. Wednesday had a poor record at Portman Road so a defeat would not arouse suspicion. Wednesday were beaten 2-0, with Swan always insisting he gave his best in the fixture. It was the catalyst for the whole affair going to court. After a trial that made national headlines, Gauld was imprisoned for four years for his match-fixing offences and given a £5,000 fine, while Layne and a third Swindon player, Jack Fountain, also went to prison after Swindon's defeat by Vale was found to be one of the games involved in Gauld's match-fixing ring. All were given a life ban from football. The ban was eventually rescinded in time for Layne to attempt to stage a comeback with Wednesday, but he didn't make the first team and ended up on loan at Hereford United before finishing with the pro game.

GOING UP (PART ONE): 1962/63

Swindon had spent more than forty years in Division Three or Division Three (South) by the start of the 1962/63 season. Manager Bert Head had patiently spent the previous seasons putting together a youthful squad by scouring the West Country for local talent. He had no qualms about giving the young players a chance to shine. The side became known as 'Bert's Babes' and included an England under-23 player in Ernie Hunt, future England international Mike Summerbee, a young John Trollope and Bobby Woodruff, who went on to play for Wolves. A promising winger called Don Rogers made his breakthrough into the first team. At the back 38-year-old Maurice Owen, such a prolific striker, provided the experience, playing in defence in his final season. There were several emphatic home wins, Colchester United were crushed 6-1, Brighton & Hove Albion and Queens Park Rangers also had five put past them. A bad winter saw a huge fixture backlog, meaning there were eight games to be played in April. At that point, Swindon were top of the table but there was a worrying run of just one win in five games after beating Bradford Park Avenue. Swindon finished the season strongly, claiming seven points out of eight in games with Bournemouth, Carlisle United, Halifax Town and Colchester United. It meant that a victory in the last home game of the season would wrap up promotion and despite being nervous as kittens, one of Head's crop of home-grown talent, Roger Smart, managed to conjure up a winner with just two minutes to go. A crowd of more than 20,000 could celebrate the prospect of Division Two football for the first time in the club's history. It completed the club's rebuilding by Bert Head, who arrived in October 1956 just after Swindon had finished bottom of Division Three (South) and needed to seek re-election. Ernie Hunt finished as top scorer with 27 goals.

Division Three Final Table

	P	W	D	L	GF	GA	PTS
1. Northampton Town (C)	**46**	**26**	**10**	**10**	**109**	**60**	**62**
2. Swindon Town (P)	**46**	**22**	**14**	**10**	**87**	**56**	**58**
3. Port Vale	46	23	8	15	72	58	54
4. Coventry City	46	18	17	11	83	69	53

OUR PATHS NEVER CROSS

Swindon have gone 23 years without meeting Preston North End in a competitive fixture, the longest gap between a match against any of the other 91 Football League teams in the 2008/9 season. The last encounter, to date, was a 3-0 win for Swindon at Deepdale on the march to the Division Four title on February 22nd 1986 which saw goals for Chris Ramsey, Charlie Henry and Peter Coyne. Since then, Swindon have played in every division of the league yet have managed to dodge North End in both league and cup games.

FROM FLOP TO FEARSOME PREDATOR

Swindon spent a then club record £500,000 on signing the Norwegian international striker Jan Age Fjortoft from Austrian side Rapid Vienna in the summer of 1993 as they prepared for their first season in the top flight of English football. With half the campaign gone, it looked like a disaster. Fjortoft struggled to adapt to English football, and went 23 games without scoring. The lowlight was a miss from virtually on the goal line against Aston Villa. Swindon brought in Andy Mutch and Keith Scott to provide the firepower that looked to be lacking and Fjortoft was confined to the bench. With his World Cup place in jeopardy, Fjortoft was close to returning to Norwegian club Lillestrom on loan. Then on January 18th 1994, came the breakthrough, when Fjortoft scored at last, in an FA Cup replay at Ipswich Town. His double clenched fist celebration indicated relief more than anything else. Fjortoft then proceeded to prove football was a confidence game, scoring 12 goals in the next 16 league matches, providing some of Town's most memorable Premier League moments in the process. Fjortoft netted in a victory over Spurs, hit a hat-trick in the win over Coventry City, notched Swindon's late equaliser against Manchester United and a spectacular goal to surprise title-chasing Blackburn Rovers at Ewood Park. If his second goal at Manchester City had been allowed who knows how Town's season might have gone. Fjortoft also developed a gleeful aeroplane celebration to mark his goals. He excelled in the League Cup next season but was sold by Steve McMahon on deadline day for just £1.3m to Middlesbrough, a move which helped condemn Town to a second straight relegation. The Norwegian remains a cult Swindon hero – and rightly so!

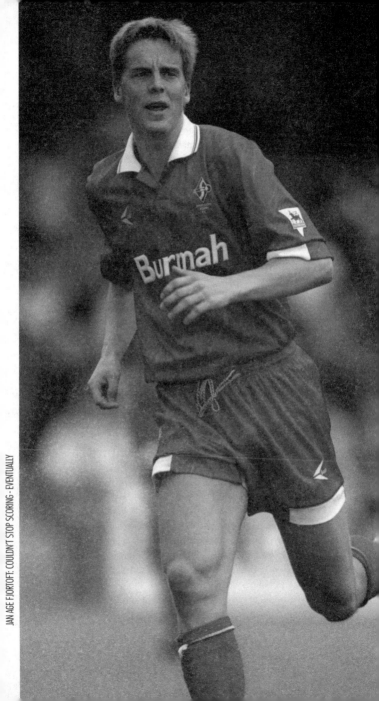

TOWN ON THE TV

Swindon have featured in three different 'fly on the wall' football documentaries. In 1963, Swindon were followed by the cameras in the build up to the game with Leyton Orient called *Six Days to Saturday*. The film was directed by John Boorman, who later went on to direct *Excalibur* and *Deliverance* and who was then part of a BBC TV documentary unit in Bristol, capturing a youthful Swindon side enjoying life in Division Two. The presence of the cameras clearly inspired Bert Head's side, who took Orient apart 5-0 in the climactic game at the end of the week. Swindon's promotion-winning side of 1993 were captured in a Channel 4 documentary called *That's Football*, made by Carl Ross. It showed a real cross section of life at Swindon. Among the best bits was a Glenn Hoddle finishing exercise during training. With the players struggling to do what was asked of them, Hoddle stepped up, casually bent the ball round the keeper to show how it was done, leaving John Moncur to look into the camera as if to say: "Are us mortals meant to be able to do that?" More recently, former boss Iffy Onuora initially featured in Sky's documentary *Big Ron Manager*, a mixture of behind-the-scenes footage based on the premise of Ron Atkinson being a figurehead to offer advice and opinions. The project appeared ill-fated from the start when there was confusion over whether Atkinson had joined Swindon as a club-appointed consultant or merely as part of the documentary. With Onuora unhappy the filming was ended after around a month, with Peterborough United ending up as the featured team.

A CLOSET SWINDON SUPPORTER?

You might have wondered if David Holdsworth had a secret affection for the Robins after scoring two own goals for Swindon against Sheffield United in three seasons. In February 1997 Holdsworth's full length diving header put Swindon 2-0 up against the Blades, and although the defender netted for his own team, Town held on to win 2-1 at the County Ground. In August 1998, he was at it again – this time scoring for Swindon at Bramall Lane, although the Blades did win. To be fair to anyone doubting his professionalism, Holdsworth did manage to confine himself to only scoring at the right end in a 2-1 United victory sandwiched in between those two matches.

SON OF MY FATHER: PART ONE

Mike and Nicky Summerbee's careers both followed an identical path in beginning at Swindon before moving to Manchester City. Mike made his Swindon debut when he was 16 back in 1959, helping Town to their first-ever promotion before City paid more than £30,000 for him in 1965 after relegation back into Division Three. He went on to play for England eight times. Son Nicky had trials at Manchester United, Leicester City and Norwich City before joining Swindon, where he was part of the side that beat the Foxes in the play-off final, and a regular in the Premier League. For a time he played in the same right wing position as his father – as well as spending time at right back. The two even had a similar running style, as if an invisible bag of coal was slung over the right shoulder. Though he never won a full England cap, Summerbee junior did play in a 'B' international before, like his dad, joining Manchester City, for a fee of more than £1m following relegation from the Premier League. He returned to Swindon to play one game in 2005 under Andy King, but a longer deal to stay never materialised.

FRAGILE GLASS SPARKLES BUT ONCE

Keeper Jimmy Glass had a pretty modest Swindon career and failed to see eye-to-eye with either of his managers, but his name is secure in football legend for one act while on Town's books – albeit not for Swindon. Glass had a tough act to follow, as he was signed by Steve McMahon after releasing Fraser Digby in 1998. He played just four games in that season and was publically criticised by boss Jimmy Quinn. At the end of the season Carlisle United, who were facing relegation from the Football League, needed a keeper on loan. Glass was dispatched to Cumbria and turned from lower league pro to icon, by scoring when he went up for a corner in injury time to give Carlisle victory over Plymouth Argyle – a goal that kept league football in Cumbria alive and sent Scarborough into the Conference instead. Glass has admitted to having serious gambling problems during his time as a pro and has led a nomadic existence – in football and otherwise – after leaving the County Ground. He's since been an IT salesman, involved in taxi driving and had a failed comeback at non-league Lewes after problems seeing the ball clearly under floodlights.

THE HAT-TRICK OF HAT-TRICKS

When Simon Cox scored a hat-trick at Northampton Town on March 24th 2009, he became the first Swindon player to get three hat-tricks in a season in 52 years. The first came in a 3-3 draw at Hartlepool United, where Town let a three-goal lead slip. Second was less than a month later at promotion contenders Scunthorpe United, but yet again Swindon couldn't hold on to a lead. The match finished 3-3. In the final game of the sequence at Sixfields, Swindon finally won 4-3, but they survived a disallowed Northampton equaliser in the final minutes. All three hat-tricks included strikes from outside the penalty area. There was also a penalty, a header and even a finish with his chest to demonstrate the striker's versatility. The previous Swindon player to score three hat-tricks in a season was Bill Stephens in the 1946/47 campaign. He hit four in Swindon's 7-0 demolition of Aldershot on September 7th 1946 and five days later he bagged three goals in a 5-1 win at Norwich City. Stephens' third and final hat-trick of the season was part of another rout, a 5-1 victory over Torquay United at the County Ground.

SPOILING SIR STANLEY'S DAY

Swindon were the opponents when Stoke City officially opened their new Britannia Stadium in August 1997. A restricted capacity crowd of 23,000 saw Sir Stanley Matthews perform the opening ceremony. Stoke took the lead in the first half through Richard Forsyth, but Town came up with two late goals to ruin the celebrations. Wayne Allison equalised with twelve minutes to go, then two minutes later Scottish striker Chris Hay scored Swindon's winner.

A PRETTY IMPORTANT NINETY MINUTES

In the autumn of 1960, a promising young winger from Somerset had caught the eye of scouts at Swindon Town and Bristol City. Town manager Bert Head picked up the boy's father one day, took him to a game, and the youngster was duly signed up on his return. Ninety minutes or so later, Bristol City's representative turned up at the Rogers household. He was Fred Ford, a future Swindon manager, but he left disappointed. The player – who Fred was to manage – was one Don Rogers.

GIVE IT TO MORRIS!

Swindon's all-time leading scorer isn't the club's only England international Harold Fleming, or someone from the heady days of the 1980s and 1990s. The proud record is held by David 'Harry' Morris, who scored 229 goals in seven ridiculously prolific seasons in the 1920s and 30s. Morris, who cost £110 from Swansea Town in 1926, started his Town career with hat-tricks in his first two games; a 5-1 thrashing of Southend United and a 4-2 defeat of Exeter City – and barely stopped scoring. He ended up with an extraordinary 48 goals from 43 games in that season. A year later, he again beat the mark of a goal per game, scoring 44 times in 42 matches before slowing down – just slightly. Morris scored 18 hat-tricks in his Swindon career and twice found the net five times in one game, in matches against Queens Park Rangers and Norwich City. Morris, who is described as very much the penalty box predator type of striker, was finally let go in 1933 after scoring a mere 13 times. His goalscoring achievements also spread to Swindon's theatre. A tale is told of a play held in Swindon which featured an attractive young woman imploring the audience at a moment of crisis; "Oh dearie me, what shall I do, what can I do?" The audience would yell out the simple solution to any Swindon problem – "Give it to Morris!" It's said one night the great man was there in the audience – on cue – to take a bow.

NO SHIRKING FROM THE SPOT

On November 17th 1993, Wales needed to beat Romania to make the 1994 World Cup in the United States. Swindon's Paul Bodin stepped up from the spot and saw his penalty smack off the crossbar with the score at 1-1. Wales went on to lose and miss out on a trip to the finals. So, it must have taken some courage to contemplate doing the same just three days later when Swindon got a late penalty at home to Ipswich Town. With seven minutes to go and Swindon trailing 2-1, Bodin took responsibility again. This time his penalty found its usual home, in the top left hand corner of the net. It gave Swindon a point in a 2-2 draw.

THANKS FOR COMING

The lowest league crowds ever to watch Swindon in the post war era, both home and away, came in Swindon's worst season, 1983/84, when the side finished in the bottom half of Division Four. Names such as Kevin Baddeley and Nigel Gray were on the teamsheet. Chester City were heading for a bottom place finish so perhaps it's not entirely surprising just 880 could rouse themselves to head to Sealand Road in February for their game with Swindon Town. Most probably wish they hadn't bothered, as Swindon won 3-0 with Garry Nelson scoring twice and Paul Batty also netting. Then on April 17th 1986, Swindon recorded their lowest home league attendance, with just 1,681 clicking through the turnstiles to see a midweek victory over Darlington. Leigh Barnard, who later helped Swindon to back-to-back promotions, got the only goal.

NO SOCCER SUNDAY

Swindon's long-serving goalkeeper Jimmy Allan was the first professional footballer to refuse to play on a Sunday for religious reasons. Sunday games were being tried out by clubs early in 1974 with Britain on the three-day week. With Swindon struggling in Division Two, Town hoped to boost attendances by switching their game with Bolton Wanderers at the start of February at the County Ground to a Sunday. In the week beforehand, Allan said he couldn't be included in the squad. He told the *Evening Advertiser*: "I am a member of the United Free Church of Scotland and I have been brought up to regard Sunday as a day for religious activities only." Allan had discussed the matter with his parents before saying he was not available, while Swindon manager Les Allen said he respected the Scot's decision. It was a brave move by the keeper, who was just 20 at the time. Allan was having a good season, establishing himself as first choice and playing well despite Swindon's poor form. Alan Spratley, signed from Queens Park Rangers, was picked instead. Les Allen was true to his word and the Scot returned in goal for Town's next game, a defeat at Millwall, but he was soon out of the side again and replaced by Spratley. Allan's moral stand didn't stop him playing more than 400 games for his only professional club. The Scot's career was ended by a horrible broken arm in a home game with Rochdale in 1983. He was given a testimonial in 1986.

GOING UP: PART TWO – 1968/69

The 1968/69 season is always remembered for the League Cup triumph, but the Swindon squad from that campaign showed their quality, fitness and resilience by also clinching promotion into Division Two for just the second time in the club's history. Frank Burrows, a tough Scottish centre-back, was signed from Scunthorpe United in the summer and his presence inspired a superb start. Keeper Peter Downsborough began the season by keeping six league clean sheets in a row, while Danny Williams' side could turn on the style at home. They put five past Southport, Tranmere Rovers and Oldham Athletic, as well as recording a 6-2 win at Northampton Town. All this was being combined with the run to the League Cup final. Perhaps not surprisingly, the two games before and one after the final were lost but things were back on track in a home game with Barnsley, when Peter Noble scored twice. Four days later, a home defeat to Watford ultimately cost Swindon the title. They were the only league side to come away from the County Ground that season with a victory. A seven game unbeaten run was a superb response, and it meant that one point was required going into the penultimate game, a Friday night match. In a gentle twist of fate, Swindon travelled to Rotherham United, the club Danny Williams served so well as a player, and then manager. Trailing 1-0 with a minute to go, Swindon put together a flowing move with Stan Harland, pushed forward, feeding substitute striker Chris Jones, who ran through and finished. Swindon played out injury time happy with the point and a place back in Division Two, with a squad that it was felt could really challenge for back-to-back promotions. Don Rogers scored an impressive 22 league goals, and Peter Noble, who went on to play in the top flight with Burnley, netted 16 times.

Divison Three Final Table

	P	W	D	L	GF	GA	PTS	GA
1. Watford (C)	46	27	10	9	74	34	64	2.18
2. Swindon Town (P)	46	27	10	9	71	35	64	2.03
3. Luton Town	46	25	11	10	74	38	61	1.95
4. Bournemouth & Bos.	46	21	9	16	60	45	51	1.33

THE ONE BLOT ON THE LANDSCAPE

Dave Mackay had a magnificent career as a player and as a manager – except at Swindon Town. Mackay, a defender widely praised for courage, heart and leadership, won the Scottish League with Hearts and was outstanding in Spurs' double-winning side of 1960/61. However, by the time the Swindon board signed him in 1971, he was in his late thirties. Mackay was effectively brought in to replace Fred Ford as manager but Ford didn't leave. Some players argue he upset the balance of the team – it saw captain Stan Harland moved into midfield and results began to worsen. When he took over as manager, the club's finances were suffering thanks to the costs of the new North Stand – and Mackay will be remembered as the man who eventually sold Don Rogers. His departure also left a sour taste. After leaving for personal reasons, Mackay was quickly unveiled as the new manager of Derby County. He rediscovered his winning touch there, leading Derby to the Division One title.

DOWN AMONG THE DEAD MEN – 1981/82

Somerton Park, the rag tag home of Newport County, is long consigned to history, yet mention of the place will always bring a wince to Swindon fans of a certain age as it's where Swindon suffered relegation into Division Four for the first time in the club's history. Swindon had only just stayed up in 1980/81 and John Trollope was forced to sell Chris Kamara and Ian Miller before the start of the season, while the popular Brian Williams was swapped for Bristol Rovers' Gary Emmanuel. The season started well though, with two big home wins; a 4-1 defeat of Wimbledon and 4-0 victory over Preston North End. Swindon actually had 20 points after ten games to be top of the table. Then a 5-0 defeat to Walsall prompted a horrible run of one win in 16 matches. As the wheels came off an inexperienced side lacked the ability to see things through, while manager Trollope was frustrated with some of the more senior pros. Teenager Paul Rideout was banging in the goals regularly though and there were encouraging signs in February and March, with a victory over Portsmouth and a 5-2 derby win over Bristol Rovers, but the goals just dried up in March and April. Rideout was the only player to score in seven games – and that was in a 5-1 home thumping by Huddersfield Town. At one point John Trollope's side were five points from safety. A 3-0 win at Bristol City, who were in free-fall, was reason for optimism. The gate was just 6,500, despite a decent travelling support. It reflected the low ebb of the two clubs and of football in general. After a defeat at Portsmouth, Swindon went to Somerton Park to face Newport County on May 18th 1982, knowing they had to win to survive. There was plenty of pressure, County keeper Kendall was in excellent form and Newport didn't seem unduly bothered. Perhaps the revenue from Swindon fans would be welcome next season. Paul Rideout hit the post from outside the penalty area. Then in the second half, Roy Carter punched away a cross and Tommy Tynan put home the penalty. Late pressure yielded nothing and Town lost 1-0 in what was Kenny Stroud's last game for the club. John Trollope admitted his young players just weren't consistent enough after years of being forced to sell many of the squad. He called it his "worst moment in football". Carter top-scored, providing 15 goals from midfield.

Division Three Final Table (bottom)

	P	W	D	L	GF	GA	PTS
19. Doncaster Rovers	46	13	17	16	55	68	56
20. Walsall	46	13	14	19	51	55	53
21. Wimbledon	46	14	11	21	61	75	53
22. Swindon Town	46	13	13	20	55	71	52
23. Bristol City	46	11	13	22	40	65	46
24. Chester City	46	7	11	28	36	78	32

THE MATCH-DAY EXPERIENCE MANY MOONS AGO

Watching a Swindon game pre-war was a very different experience. Pre-match entertainment would consist of a brass band marching through the town centre and onto the County Ground pitch, eventually stopping in the centre circle to perform. With no tannoy, the crowd were informed of team changes by a man with a chalk board who would walk round the perimeter of the pitch, listing any alterations from the programme for the crowd to see. The only seating normally available was in the Main Stand at the side of the ground closest to the cricket pitch but for big games, extra fans were allowed to sit on benches on the cinder track that surrounded the pitch. At half-time, people would throw money into a sheet carried round the pitch, with the cash going to local charities.

TRANSFER INFLATION

Swindon signings which broke various financial landmarks:

Oct 1937......... Ben Morton......................£1,000 from Torquay United
Nov 1947........ Morris Jones ....£2,500 from Port Vale
Aug 1959........ Jimmy Gauld ....£6,500 from Plymouth Argyle
Mar 1964........ Frank Large ....£10,000 from Queens Park Rangers
Nov 1964........ Dennis Brown ....£15,000 from Chelsea
May 1971........ Dave Mackay...................£20,000 from Derby County
Jun 1972.......... Ray Treacy...................£35,000 from Charlton Athletic
Nov 1972........ Tommy Jenkins.................£50,000 from Southampton
Dec 1979 .... Glen Cockerill ....£110,000 from Lincoln
Mar 1980........ David Peach.....................£150,000 from Southampton
Jun 1988.......... Duncan Shearer...............£250,000 from Huddersfield
Dec 1990 .... Nestor Lorenzo ....£400,000 from Bari
Jul 1993...........Jan Age Fjortoft.............£500,000 from Rapid Vienna
Jul 1994........... Mark Robinson ....£600,000 from Newcastle
Aug 1994........Joey Beauchamp .....£800,000 from West Ham United

CULLING A CAREER BEFORE IT STARTED

Swindon played their part in what was perhaps the most surreal managerial appointment ever seen in the Football League. Swansea City had announced Kevin Cullis was to be their manager in 1996. His entire management experience appeared to consist of managing the youth team at Cradley Town, a small non-league side in the Midlands. Swindon turned up at the Vetch Field for his first game and won 1-0 on their way to the Division Two title courtesy of a Shaun Taylor goal. Cullis was gone inside a week.

TWO STRIKES AT GLORY

Swindon's first post-war manager Louis Page was an England football international, winning seven caps as a forward in the 1920s. He also represented England in another sport – as he was a talented baseball player. Page played baseball with brother Tom, who was also a professional footballer in the winter months.

NOT ALWAYS RED AND WHITE

Swindon's colours are very much traditionally seen as red and white, but in its very early days the club had several different strips. After becoming known as Swindon Town, the first kit was red and black quarters with black shorts. Then there came a period of wearing green and white, before a change into maroon, which was caused by a struggle to get the green dye required. The more scarlet red has been the main colour since World War I. The red kit appears to have been the prompt for the 'Robins' nickname. The 1970s saw a flirtation with the club logo being on the centre of the shirt and a spell wearing black shorts. Since then the shorts have alternated between being white and red. The away kits have been in a whole host of shades. The author's own personal favourite was the dark blue and black halves of 1995/96, while the most hilarious was undoubtedly the green and white 'potato print' design of 1992/93. Luckily, concentrating on the quality of the football made it much more bearable.

CHAMPIONS: PART ONE – 1985/86

Swindon have twice won divisional championships since their entry into the Football League in 1920, but they had to wait for 66 years to lift a first title, when Lou Macari's side ended up romping through Division Four in 1985/86. Macari made one of the best signings in Swindon history when he signed Scottish defender Colin Calderwood from Mansfield Town for £27,500 in 1985 but the campaign actually started slowly, with two wins from the first eight games. The arrival of experienced keeper Kenny Allen from Torquay United helped stabilise things and it was lift-off from October onwards. A 1-0 win at Torquay just after Christmas moved Swindon to the top of the table for the first time and a defeat against Tranmere Rovers in January was to be Town's last, with a club record 21-match unbeaten league run seeing Swindon take the title. It included six straight away victories from January to March, with no home game due to bad weather. Dave Bamber was signed for £15,000 from Portsmouth after a loan spell earlier in the season and he scored in a record-breaking fourteenth home league win in a row over Burnley. Swindon had the chance to clinch promotion at home against Chester City, who were their closest rivals for the title. The 12,630 crowd at the County Ground saw Swindon fall behind early as Steve Johnson capitalised on Kenny Allen's weak punch from a corner. Dave Bamber headed in Dave Hockaday's cross for an equaliser, but right on half-time Chester won a penalty, that Johnson had to take twice – and scored twice. The second half saw a fantastic turnaround with two goals in three minutes in front of the Town End; headers from Dave Bamber and Bryan Wade. Leigh Barnard got the fourth and Swindon could afford to miss a penalty late on. The final whistle sparked a pitch invasion. The championship arrived with a 1-1 draw at Mansfield and going into the last game, at home to Crewe, a win would take Swindon to 102 points, a then-league record. The Alex held out for 70 minutes, before Peter Coyne scored the only goal of the game. A premature pitch invasion delayed the final whistle, but the season ended in perfect fashion with Colin Calderwood and Lou Macari, sacked the season before, lifting the Division Four trophy. Charlie Henry ended up as top scorer, with 18 goals. The campaign saw 17 different club records broken or matched.

Division Four Final Table

	P	W	D	L	GF	GA	PTS	GD
1. Swindon Town (C)	46	32	6	8	82	43	102	+39
2. Chester City (P)	46	23	15	8	83	50	84	+33
3. Mansfield Town (P)	46	23	12	11	74	47	81	+27
4. Port Vale (P)	46	21	16	9	67	37	79	+30
5. Orient	46	20	12	14	79	64	72	+15
6. Colchester United	46	19	13	14	88	63	70	+25

VISIONARY IDEA

Swindon were one of the early trendsetters in 1951 in installing floodlights, albeit the idea was inspired by a trip to Headington United. They cost £350 and were tried out for the first time in a friendly with Bristol City on April 2nd. A crowd of just over three thousand turned up despite a downpour and the idea was declared a tentative success, even though the heavy rain limited visibility and the white ball used quickly became coated with mud. Sixteen 1,500 watt lamps were used to illuminate the pitch. Swindon won the match 2-1, with Scottish winger William Millar scoring in each half, but it was thought the main use for the lights would be to allow training in the evening, rather than play competitive matches at night.

THE GREATEST ROBIN OF THEM ALL?

Harold Fleming is the only player to ever play for England while at Swindon and this was in the days when Town were in the Southern League. Fleming, an inside-forward, made his debut at the age of 20 in 1908, scoring against Luton Town. A record of 28 goals in 34 games earned him his England call-up in 1909 for a match against Scotland, and he netted three goals in two internationals in June of that year against Hungary. He went on to win 11 caps, scoring 9 goals, including a hat-trick in February 1912 when England beat Ireland 6-1 in Dublin. Fleming was also central to Swindon's best-ever FA Cup runs, two trips to the semi-finals in 1908 and 1912, while he was top scorer when Swindon won the Southern League in the 1910/11 season. During World War I he worked as a PT instructor in Cambridge and he resumed his Swindon career afterwards, playing for Town in their first ever game in the Football League's newly created Third Division. His last game for the club came in 1924, and naturally he scored, in a 4-0 win over Brighton & Hove Albion. It was the final one of 206 goals in 337 games for the Robins. In the 1920s Fleming was filmed giving a football 'masterclass' in the days before sound, to a background of piano music. The footage was recently discovered by Swindon fan James Turner after being put up for sale on eBay. It shows, among other things, how to play 'The Triangular Game' to keep possession. Fleming, who was spotted by Swindon playing for local church side St. Mark's, would not play on Christmas Day or on Good Friday. After his retirement he ran a sports outfitters shop in Regent's Circus until his death in 1955. A road into the heart of Swindon, Fleming Way, was named in his honour, while a bust of Fleming is in the County Ground reception.

IT'S NEVER TOO LATE TO START

Swindon's oldest ever debutant is, predictably, a goalkeeper. Scot Alex Ferguson (not that one) made his debut on September 13th 1947 from Bristol City, having been signed up at the age of 44. He made seven league appearances. The oldest outfield debutant is a recent one, Paul Ince, who played his three games for Swindon at the age of 38.

WHY THE MEN OF KENT CAN'T FORGIVE

A rivalry between Swindon and Gillingham wouldn't have much logic to it. I suppose Gillingham have always been looking for a natural enemy, only having had Maidstone United as another Kent side in the league – and that all too briefly. However, among Gills supporters, especially of a certain generation, there appears to be a festering dislike of Swindon. It stems back to two matches back in the second half of the 1978/79 season with both teams going for promotion. Firstly, Swindon recovered from a 2-0 deficit in their meeting at the Priestfield to make it 2-2. Gillingham striker Danny Westwood was then sent off after a clash with Ray McHale. Further decisions from referee David Hutchinson so infuriated the natives that later on in the game one of them ran on to the Priestfield pitch and felled him with a punch. McHale was seen as the villain by the men from Kent. The return game at the County Ground – again with both teams still bang in contention for promotion – saw the Gills' Terry Nicholl sent off by Lester Shapter for two fouls on Ray McHale, and Town went on to win 3-1 in a game that turned pretty ugly, with McHale insisting he was a "target" for the Gills players after the match. After the game was over, a number of Gillingham players were subsequently questioned by the police over incidents in the tunnel that saw coach Wilf Tranter taken to hospital. Ken Price and Dean White went to court over the incident, were found guilty and given a conditional discharge. Gillingham went on to miss promotion by one point, with Swindon finishing just below then in fifth. Add Swindon beating the Gills in the 1987 play-offs and their frustration has simmered for more than 20 years.

SQUAD FOR SALE

The 1983/84 season was one of the bleakest in Swindon history. The club recorded its worst Football League finish of 17th in Division Four, with home attendances dropping to below 2,000 on a number of occasions. Swindon were trapped in the vicious circle of poor results, falling gates and low income. It meant the entire squad was put on the transfer list before the campaign was out. Manager Ken Beamish told *HTV*: "I'll sell any of them. If any offer comes in it will be considered."

INTERNATIONALS IN CHARGE

Fourteen different former internationals have managed Swindon Town. The first was Ted Vizard, a Welshman who was an outside-left at Bolton Wanderers. He was appointed in 1933. There have been five Scottish internationals; Neil Harris, Dave Mackay, Lou Macari, Paul Sturrock and Maurice Malpas, and five Englishmen amongst them; Louis Page, Glenn Hoddle, Steve McMahon, Colin Todd and Dennis Wise. Two have played for Northern Ireland; Jimmy Quinn and current boss Danny Wilson, with Argentinian Ossie Ardiles completing the set.

BLUES GIVE REDS THE BLUES

In 1960, part of the pre-season build-up under manager Bert Head, as was tradition, was playing the likely first choice XI in a game open to the public at the County Ground. The established players were 'the Reds' and the up-and-coming hopefuls 'the Blues'. The Blues were given a bit of assistance by Maurice Owen. A few eyebrows were raised when the 'Blues' went on to beat the senior side 7-2 with Ken Mellor scoring a hat-trick. The seniors included Mike Summerbee, Ernie Hunt and Bronco Layne. The youngsters went on to win a second game behind closed doors. It meant when the season started against Halifax Town, Swindon played with a pair of 17-year-old full backs in John Trollope and Terry Wollen. Bert Head preferred them to the on-trial players he looked at, Bell and Richardson, who had been humbled by the youngsters. It's thought to be the youngest full-back pairing in Football League history.

TALKATIVE TED

The Swindon Town goalkeeper of the 1920s Ted Nash was clearly a relaxed sort. Fans can remember him chatting cheerily to supporters behind his goal when Swindon were on the attack! Nash, who played more than 200 games for Swindon in an 11-year Robins career, doubled up as a wicketkeeper for Wiltshire. After marrying the Swindon ladies' keeper, he actually ended up working for Sussex County Cricket Club, keeping an eye on the dressing rooms. Perhaps his finest game for Swindon was in January 1930, when Town pulled off a 2-0 win at Manchester United in the FA Cup with Nash in excellent form as he produced a string of saves to keep United at bay.

GOAL MACHINES

Simon Cox's two goals against Bristol Rovers on April 25th 2009 made him the seventh Swindon player to hit thirty goals in a Football League season. Duncan Shearer's efforts are all the more impressive given he was sold to Blackburn Rovers on transfer deadline day.

Simon Cox.................32.....................2008/09
29 League, 1 FA Cup, 2 Others
Duncan Shearer.........32.....................1991/92
22 League, 4 FA Cup, 6 League Cup
Jimmy Quinn.............31.....................1987/88
21 League, 8 League Cup, 2 Others
Peter Eastoe..............31.....................1974/75
26 League, 5 FA Cup
Don Rogers................30.....................1968/69
22 League, 1 FA Cup, 7 League Cup
Don Rogers................32.....................1966/67
24 League, 7 FA Cup, 1 League Cup
Ben Morton...............32.....................1938/39
28 League, 3 FA Cup, 1 Other
Harry Morris.............35.....................1930/31
35 League
Harry Morris.............31.....................1928/29
26 League, 5 FA Cup
Harry Morris.............44.....................1927/28
38 League, 6 FA Cup
Harry Morris.............48.....................1926/27
47 League, 1 FA Cup

A NARROW ESCAPE

The home game with Plymouth Argyle in the Southern League in January 1920 nearly ended in tragedy. Fire broke out in the back of the grandstand and it took some prompt police action, asking some fans to move, plus swift work procuring several buckets of water, to make sure the fire didn't quickly spread. An estimated crowd of 10,000 was present, with the game not stopped at any stage. Most people were too absorbed in a 2-1 Swindon win.

CLOSE BUT NO CIGAR

Every club seems to have a striker who achieves something between cult status and infamy for his inability to score. For Swindon that man is Shaun Close, who managed just two goals in 53 appearances. Close was signed in September 1989 from Bournemouth having begun life at Spurs. After a blank first season, Close finally got on the score-sheet against Division Four Darlington in a 1990 League Cup game, helping Town overturn a 3-0 first leg deficit. His one solitary league strike was more than a year later. To be fair at least it was at a good place, the Manor Ground, though it was in a 5-3 defeat. Close was finally released in 1993 after four undistinguished seasons. He then had an equally non-prolific spell at Barnet, before ending up running a pub.

THE ULTIMATE SACRIFICE

Swindon players died in both World War I and World War II serving their country. Second Lieutenant Freddy Wheatcroft, a prolific scorer in the Southern League for Swindon, was part of the East Surrey Regiment and was killed in battle in 1917, at the age of 35. He is buried at the Anneux Cemetery in the north of France. World War II claimed the lives of two players, Alan Fowler, and James Olney. Fowler, a prolific scorer in wartime football, lost his life in July 1944, while Olney had joined the Coldstream Guards. A third, William Imrie, is listed on a plaque at the club, but research by Swindon historian Paul Plowman has cast doubt as to whether or not he died in action.

GOING UP: PART THREE 1986/87

After the record-breaking season of 1985/86, Lou Macari set about improving his squad for a crack at Division Three in the 1986/87 season. His early recruits were a striker called Steve White, seemingly not wanted at Bristol Rovers, where Bobby Gould suggested he play part-time and work in the community department, while another Gashead, Tim Parkin, was brought into central defence. An early 6-2 defeat by Blackpool saw keeper Kenny Allen dropped and the Manchester United youngster Fraser Digby arrived on loan. Digby's arrival saw a run of six wins in eight games, including a superb ding-dong 4-3 win at Port Vale. Lou Macari made another significant signing in December, paying £50,000 to bring Jimmy Quinn back to the County Ground, while also completing Digby's permanent move. After a defeat at Chester on April Fools' Day there was a strong finish to the season – 11 matches unbeaten – but several draws meant it wasn't enough to catch AFC Bournemouth and Middlesbrough in the top two promotion places. The play-offs saw a semi-final with Wigan Athletic and Swindon were 2-0 behind inside 15 minutes at Springfield Park. In the last half-hour, though, the Macari fitness regime told. Dave Bamber made it 2-1 and Jimmy Quinn headed in a free kick to make it 2-2 before Peter Coyne completed the comeback. The second leg finished 0-0 with Wigan hitting the post and Dave Bamber having a late goal disallowed. It meant a two-legged final with Gillingham, who had sent Sunderland down. The Gills won the first leg 1-0 and Karl Elsey's spectacular volley at the County Ground meant Macari's side had to chase down a 2-0 deficit. Swindon battered away and got the first goal back through Peter Coyne. With less than 15 minutes left Charlie Henry, top scorer the previous season, but out of favour, smacked a terrific volley past Phil Kite to level things up. It meant the tie finished 2-2. There was no 'away goals' rule and a third match was needed. The two sides met at Selhurst Park and on a raucous night in south London Steve White scored right at the start of the match, tucking home Henry's flick on. It was Swindon's quickest goal of the season. White's persistence got the second and after a marathon campaign, it was back-to-back promotions. For White, it probably beat setting up a few soccer schools. He shared the honour of being top scorer with Dave Bamber – both netted 21 goals.

Divison Three Final Table

	P	W	D	L	GF	GA	PTS
1. AFC Bournemouth (C)	**46**	**29**	**10**	**7**	**76**	**40**	**97**
2. Middlesbrough (P)	**46**	**28**	**10**	**8**	**67**	**30**	**94**
3. Swindon Town (P)	46	25	12	9	77	47	87
4. Wigan Athletic	46	25	10	11	83	60	85
5. Gillingham	46	23	9	14	65	48	78
6. Bristol City	46	21	14	11	63	36	77

IRISH EYES ARE SMILING

Here's a Swindon side made up of Irishmen, from north and south of the border, playing in a 4-4-2 formation with Jimmy Quinn taking a player-manager role.

Norman Uprichard ....goalkeeper.......................................1949/52
Wayne O'Sullivan ....right-back 1992/97
Alan McDonald ....centre-back 1997/98
Roy Walsh ....centre-back 1980/81
Colin Bailie.........................left-back..1982/85
Trevor Anderson ....left wing 1974/77
Kevin Horlock.....................central midfield.............................1992/97
Alan McLoughlin ....central midfield.............................1986/90
Harry Lunn ....right midfield................................1948/54
Ray Treacy ....striker 1972/73
Jimmy Quinn ....striker .... 1981/84, 1986/88 and 1998/00

WORLD CUP ROBINS

Swindon have had two players who took part in a World Cup while part of the County Ground playing staff. In 1990 Alan McLoughlin, fresh from his Wembley winner, was part of Jack Charlton's Republic of Ireland squad who made the last eight in Italy. McLoughlin came off the bench in Ireland's first two group games, draws with England and Egypt. Four years later striker Jan Age Fjortoft was part of Egil Olsen's Norway squad. He started in a win over Mexico and defeat by Italy but couldn't reproduce his prolific Swindon form in front of goal. Norway managed to finish bottom of their group despite picking up four points and Fjortoft was flying home. Argentinian defender Nestor Lorenzo, meanwhile, signed for Swindon just months after being on the losing side in the 1990 World Cup final.

THE DALE ALWAYS FAIL

The name of Swindon Town should bring a cold shiver of fear to Rochdale fans. Dale have yet to beat Swindon in 13 attempts stretching back to an FA Cup meeting in 1911. The record stands at nine wins for Swindon and four draws.

NOW WHAT WAS I MEANT TO DO?

On April 9th 2002, Swindon completed a fairly routine win over Cambridge United at the Abbey Stadium. Andy Gurney scored one and made one in a 2-1 victory – Town were in mid-table and the U's doomed to relegation. The local press corps dutifully waited around for the verdict of manager Andy King – and they waited some more. However, just when they'd given up hope King emerged – from an unexpected direction, admitting he'd driven a couple of miles from the ground before remembering he was required for an interview!

HE WASN'T THAT BAD?

Swindon's 3-1 win over Burnley on March 15th 1986 is mainly remembered as the game which broke a club record, as it was a fourteenth straight league victory at home. It's also remembered by the Burnley defender Jim Heggarty, as the Clarets' team coach left afterwards without him! Town manager Lou Macari phoned the police and the coach was diverted back to the County Ground to pick him up.

I REMEMBER YOU... JUST

Eight players have made a minimal impact on Swindon history by making just one senior appearance as substitute. The briefest belongs to striker Alex Meechan, who came on as an injury-time sub in a 3-1 defeat at Wolves on October 18th 1997. Meechan got three more chances on the bench but never came on. However, he wins the ultimate one-game wonder award. The other seven are keepers Matt Bulman and Alan Flanagan, plus strikers John Sutton, Marcus Phillips, Peter Dornan, Phil Harris and Ian Farr.

THE TWELFTH MAN

Owen Dawson was the first Swindon player ever to be used as a substitute. He came on with five minutes left of Swindon's defeat at Southend United on September 24th 1965, replacing the injured Ken Skeen in a game Swindon lost 4-2. Right-back Dawson spent nine seasons with Swindon before leaving to go to South Africa.

NO MAGIC OF THE FA CUP: PART ONE

When Ian Culverhouse was red-carded for handball in Swindon's FA Cup tie at Goodison Park against Everton in January 1997 he set a new record for the fastest sending-off in the competition proper. He was dismissed by ref Neale Barry after just 52 seconds, accused of stopping Andrei Kanchelskis' goal-bound shot with his arm, though he pleaded the ball rebounded off his chest before going over the crossbar. Kanchelskis scored from the resulting penalty and Swindon went on to lose the match 3-0 on a subdued Sunday in Merseyside.

I WANT TO BE RE-ELECTED

Swindon had to go cap in hand to the Football League three times to keep their place in the archaic act of re-election. The process took place at the league AGM on the first Saturday of each June and was often seen as an 'old boys' club', until its replacement by automatic promotion and relegation from the Conference. The first time was in 1932/33 and Swindon kept their place comfortably. In a grim spell during the 1950s, Swindon had to apply in consecutive seasons. After the 1955/56 campaign Swindon easily retained their place in the league, winning 42 votes, while their nearest challengers, Peterborough United, had just eight. Gloucester City's attempt to sneak in got but a single vote. The following year there was no need to sweat either, with Swindon again seeing off the challenge of Peterborough United, and Bedford, in their first season with Bert Head in charge.

A HELPING HAND BUT NOT ENOUGH

When Aldershot were facing extinction in 1992 two clubs offered to help the Shots out. Swindon were one of them. The old Aldershot FC had played what proved to be their last game at Cardiff City at Ninian Park on 20 March 1992. The club was in a desperate state with players not being paid and not training as they couldn't afford the travel costs, with bucket collections at matches helping to keep things going. Swindon and Cardiff both offered to stage Shots home games in an effort to keep the club going but sadly it wasn't enough to prevent the High Court winding them up shortly afterwards.

LOVING THE LEAGUE CUP: PART TWO: 1979/80

Just over a decade after Swindon's finest hour in lifting the 1969 League Cup, Bobby Smith's Town came remarkably close to going back to Wembley as a Third Division side again in the 1979/80 season; and again, spookily enough, Arsenal were beaten. The first two rounds saw Town record aggregate wins over Fourth Division Portsmouth and Division Three side Chester City. Round three saw Swindon beat top flight Stoke City. After a 2-2 draw at the Victoria Ground goals from Ray McHale and Alan Mayes gave Swindon a 2-1 win. A kind draw was the reward, as Wimbledon were seen off in round four at Plough Lane to set up a quarter-final at Arsenal. Substitute Billy Tucker headed a late equaliser at Highbury from a corner after Alan Sunderland's first-half penalty gave the home side the lead. Tucker found himself playing for the reserves 24 hours later. The replay is one of the all-time classic matches at the County Ground. Steve Walford more than played his part, heading into his own net to put Swindon 1-0 up, before Alan Mayes shot deflected off him to make it 2-0. Liam Brady scored for Arsenal before another own goal, this time from John Hollins, restored a two-goal lead. But, Brady got a second, and with six minutes to go Brian Talbot nodded home the equaliser that sent the match into extra time. With Kenny Stroud asked to mark Brady out of the match Swindon re-asserted themselves and Andy Rowland scored with just four minutes of extra time left to take Town into the last four. The semi-final saw Swindon up against a Wolves side who included Andy Gray in their squad. In the first leg Andy Rowland headed home Chris Kamara's cross, Peter Daniel equalised, but Alan Mayes late goal gave Swindon a one-goal lead to take to Molineux. Despite another win over top flight opponents Swindon were disappointed with the performance, if not the result. The second leg remains full of 'ifs' and 'what might have beens'. Firstly, Billy Tucker had a goal disallowed. Two goals in quick succession put Wolves in control on the night, but then there was a moment that surely would have had greater repercussions if it had happened today. Keeper Paul Bradshaw clattered into Alan Mayes in the chase for a ball over the top, leaving him needing stitches in a nasty facial injury. Bradshaw was only booked – remember, this is an era of no substitute keepers – and Ray McHale tucked the resulting penalty past him. A nakedly physical Wolves side clinched the tie when Jimmy Allan couldn't hold on to Andy Gray's shot and Mel Eves finished from close range to deny Swindon a Wembley final with Brian Clough's Nottingham Forest.

FACTS AND FIGURES: LEAGUE CUP 1979/80

Round/Scorers	Opponents	Score
First round first leg	Portsmouth (A)	1-1
Rowland		
First round second leg	Portsmouth (H)	2-0
Mellor (og), Carter		
Second round first leg	Chester City (H)	1-0
Mayes		
Second round second leg	Chester City (A)	1-1
Mayes		
Third round	Stoke City (A)	2-2
Mayes, Rowland		
Third round replay	Stoke City (H)	2-1
McHale, Mayes		
Fourth round	Wimbledon (A)	2-1
Rowland, Bates		
Quarter-final	Arsenal (A)	1-1
Tucker		
Quarter-final replay	Arsenal (H)	4-3
Walford (og), Mayes, Hollins (og), Rowland		
Semi-final first leg	Wolverhampton Wanderers (H)	2-1
Mayes, Rowland		
Semi-final second leg	Wolverhampton Wanderers (A)	1-3
McHale (pen)		

FROM RUSSIA, WITH LOVE

Swindon did their bit for Cold War relations in November 1972, when they hosted Russian top flight side Leningrad Zenit as part of a four-match tour of England. Swindon, playing a full-strength team, beat the former Russian Cup winners 4-2 with a spell of three goals in 13 minutes. Peter Noble, Roger Smart, Steve Peplow and David Dangerfield were the scorers.

NOT A PEACH OF A SIGNING

Southampton full-back David Peach was not a big success when Swindon paid out £150,000 for him in March 1980. The left-back was signed by Bobby Smith to replace John Trollope, a nigh on impossible task. Peach was brought in on big money and this may well have unsettled the players around him. Perhaps the only thing the FA Cup-winner got out of his spell at Swindon was travel. After completing his move from Swindon to Orient after two unhappy years, Peach went on to become the first player to play on all 92 league grounds.

SOME SECOND HALF

Swindon were at home to Charlton Athletic in August 1969 in an early game in their Division Two campaign. At half-time it was nil-nil. That was to change in spectacular style as Swindon produced a rampant second-half display with Don Rogers involved in all five goals. John Smith touched in Rogers' corner for the first, and his low ball found Peter Noble for number two. Rogers then picked out the overlapping John Trollope for number three, which was an own goal off Jack Burkett as Trollope hared into the penalty area. Rogers and Trollope worked their magic again from a corner which Noble finished to make it 4-0. Noble then got his hat-trick smashing in Rogers' deflected cross to complete a vintage afternoon's entertainment for the Town End. All five goals came in the space of 35 minutes.

BAD LIGHT STOPS PLAY

In the 1900/01 season Swindon had a poor campaign in Division One of the Southern League. They finished one off the bottom of the table, with only Chatham, who failed to complete the season, below them. It meant a play-off with Brentford, known as a Test match. The game at Reading went into extra time with the score at 0-0. With no floodlights in those days though, the game was abandoned soon afterwards due to bad light, as good a way as any a Test match to end. With Chatham folding and Gravesend leaving, the league decided that both clubs could play in Division One next season, saving Swindon from the drop.

THE ANGLO-ITALIAN CUP

Swindon are surely unique in having a cup competition created for their benefit. Town were not entered into the 1970 Uefa Cup, despite winning the League Cup, due to their relatively lowly league status. As a consolation, Swindon got to play Roma in the grandly titled Anglo-Italian League Cup Winners' Cup, a two-legged game with the then Italian cup holders. Swindon won the tie 5-2 on aggregate, with summer signing Arthur Horsfield hitting a hat-trick in a superb 4-0 win at the County Ground. The event was enough of a success to prompt an end-of-season Anglo-Italian Cup, featuring six teams from each nation. There's more on Swindon's 1970 win elsewhere in the book. The competition lasted for four seasons. It was then revived in 1992 as a competition between English and Italian second-tier clubs to replace the Full Members Cup – with Town involved in the preliminary stages. Swindon did have brief memories of their 1970s Italian adventures in the 1994/95 edition, playing Ascoli and Venezia away, and Lecce and Atalanta at home. The competition lasted just four seasons before ending in 1996. Despite a Wembley final, interest was low and the Anglo-Italian Cup shows no signs of being revived.

BACK OF THE NET

Here are Swindon's all-time top-ten goalscorers in peacetime matches. Without World War II, striker Alan Fowler would surely have made this list:

Harry Morris	229
Harold Fleming	206
Don Rogers	181
Maurice Owen	165
Archie Bown	142
Steve White	111
Andy Rowland	98
Duncan Shearer	98
Freddy Wheatcroft	98
Ernie Hunt	88

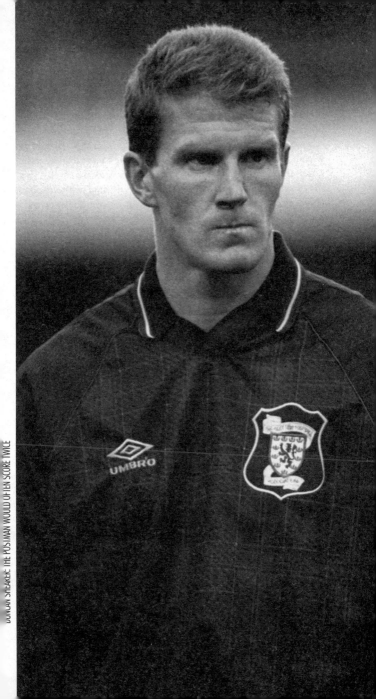

SON OF MY FATHER: PART TWO

While Mike and Nicky Summerbee were both big successes, other sons of well known Swindon players have attempted to follow their father's career route with less success. John Trollope's son Paul earned a pro contract with Swindon but failed to make a first team appearance in the Glenn Hoddle era. However, he went on to have a more than successful career as a midfielder, becoming a Welsh international and playing in the Premier League for Derby County. He's currently first team coach at Bristol Rovers. David Stroud, the son of popular 1970s defender Kenny, played three games for Town as a winger but was released by Paul Sturrock while Charlie Henry's son, Leigh, made the bench for the first team but not a senior appearance. At present, Billy Bodin, son of full-back Paul, is part of the youth set up as a striker.

WHY DOES IT ALWAYS RAIN ON ME?

Swindon were going for promotion in the 1978/79 season into Division Two as the season came to a finish in May. With Town's hopes gradually ebbing away a win was essential in the local derby with Oxford United at the start of the month. So, manager Bobby Smith wanted the pitch watered to prevent a dry, bubbly, playing service. The forecast said a few showers of rain were likely but no more, so on came the hoses – and down came the rain. By 4.30pm local referee Pete Ackrill declared the pitch unfit to play due to water-logging. After much negotiation with Oxford officials Swindon were able to stage the game twenty-four hours later. The delay had no adverse effects and Town beat their local rivals 2-0 with Chic Bates and Roy Carter scoring.

A BEVY OF BEAUTIES

The ladies of Swindon were invited to become Swindon Football Queen in a beauty contest that ran for a time in the 1960s. The 16-year-old Jacqueline Tuck, who won the third running of the competition in 1965, was reported to be so stunned by being chosen she burst into tears, while sisters Shirley and Pat Reade were also winners – in different years. Among the 1965 judges were lucky club director Len Collings and Don Pearce, the supporters' club chairman.

REDDY TO TRAVEL ANYWHERE

Ex-Swindon players have appeared all over the football pyramid, and indeed the globe, after leaving the County Ground, but striker Michael Reddy has ended up in the most unlikely of football destinations. Reddy was signed on loan from Sunderland in the 2000/01 season and was one of the better performers as Town escaped relegation, scoring five times in 20 games. Injuries meant his career never reached its potential and he ended up playing in both Greenland, and most recently the Falkland Islands, where it's reported he turns out for Port Stanley Albion.

NO MAGIC OF THE FA CUP: PART TWO

When Swindon were knocked out of the FA Cup by Barnet in January 2008 on penalties, they set another unwanted cup record by becoming the first side to miss all four penalties in an FA Cup shoot-out. Billy Paynter, who scored at both ends in the 1-1 draw at Underhill, began proceedings by hitting the bar. Christian Roberts shot wide, Hasney Aljofree's effort sailed over and when Miguel Comminges at last got a penalty on target it was saved by the Barnet keeper Rob Beckwith. You could say at least they had the bottle to step up – but then again...

A CULVERHOUSE MEANS IT'S ALL OVER

Former Swindon defender Ian Culverhouse became the centre point of one of the many strange skits that make up Sky Sports' *Soccer AM*. For a time, there would be a segment just before a commercial break. It would feature a contest, usually between two dinner-suited individuals. They'd sit opposite each other in a set up very similar to a chess match. The two contestants would name semi-famous footballers of the 1980s and 1990s, before clicking a clock, again as you would see at a world chess final. A mock analytical commentary followed the action, praising the choice or name, or expressing bewilderment from time to time. In a game with very distinct echoes of *Mornington Crescent* on Radio 4's *I'm Sorry I Haven't a Clue*, the winner was always the first person to name Ian Culverhouse, which would be followed by a volley of applause from the spectators present.

JEEPERS KEEPERS

The last twenty years have proved barren in terms of memorable cup upsets for Swindon, so perhaps what happened at Leeds United in 2003 was only to be expected. Younger readers might be shocked to know Leeds were a Premier League side when Town were given a trip to Elland Road in the Carling Cup. A glorious display put Swindon 2-0 up with 13 minutes to go, as Andy Gurney cracked home a thirty-yard free kick, and Sam Parkin made it two as Town gave a defence including Brazilian World Cup winner Roque Junior the run around. With the score 2-1, keeper Bart Griemink was sent off, and in desperation Leeds sent goalkeeper Paul Robinson up for an injury time corner. Robinson promptly headed in the equaliser and a 10-man Town side battled through extra time, only to lose on penalties.

SEVEN COSTING SEVEN FIGURES

Swindon have never spent a million pounds on a player – and nor are they likely to in the near future but seven players have left the County Ground for seven-figure sums. The first was Alan McLoughlin, who departed for £1m to Southampton in 1990. Colin Calderwood cost Spurs £1.25m in 1993, while at the end of the Premier League season John Moncur left for West Ham in a £1m deal. Nicky Summerbee fetched £1.5m from Manchester City. The following season Jan Age Fjortoft joined Middlesbrough for an insulting £1.3m. In January 1997 Kevin Horlock was also on his way to Manchester City for £1.5m, while speedy striker George Ndah completes the millionaires' row with his £1m move to Wolves.

NO ACT OF CHARITY

Swindon played their part in the highest scoring Charity/Community Shield game ever, when they were beaten 8-4 by Manchester United on September 25th 1911. At that stage, the match took place between the winners of the Football League and the Southern League, which Swindon had claimed the previous season. United striker Harold Halse scored six times in the match that was richly entertaining – it was 4-3 at half-time. Harold Fleming was among the Swindon scorers in a game played at Chelsea's Stamford Bridge, while Swindon could point to the absence of Scottish international Jock Walker in defence as one reason for their defeat.

SACKED FOR LESS THAN SEVEN DAYS

There may never quite be another managerial reign like Lou Macari's at Swindon for drama – on and off the pitch – but it was almost nipped in the bud late into his first season with the club. Macari was dismissed during Easter 1985 after relations with his assistant, Harry Gregg, became sufficiently strained for the board to demand action. Chairman Brian Hillier explained the sacking to the public by saying: "We felt we were left with no alternative because of their inability to work together." It was later claimed Gregg and Macari disagreed on the way the side should play and even that Gregg kept diaries detailing everything that went on. Fans and several players vehemently disagreed with Macari's dismissal. Striker Andy Rowland went public with his support for Macari, incurring the wrath of the club's directors. The following game with Southend United was disrupted by pitch invasions in protest, while supporters chanted and carried banners calling for Macari's re-instatement. Macari was there to watch, though Gregg wasn't. A petition with close on 1,500 signatures was delivered to the County Ground demanding his return. The board relented within a week and fan power saw Macari, genuinely touched by the support for him, get his job back, but Gregg was gone for good. The following season saw Swindon take the Fourth Division championship and start a spectacular climb through the leagues.

TWINNED

Swindon have had twins play for them – and also had two games featuring twin brothers on the opposing side. Alf and Bill Stephens arrived from Leeds United for the start of the 1946/7 season as part of the process of rebuilding the side after World War II. Striker Bill hit 26 goals in his first season before moving to West Ham United in December 1947, but Alf's stay wasn't nearly as happy as he suffered a broken leg. On September 22nd 2001, Swindon defender Alan Reeves came up against his twin brother David, a striker, as the Robins played Chesterfield. David got the opener as Town slipped to a 4-0 defeat at Saltergate. Alan got his revenge when it was Reeves v Reeves again on January 4th 2003. Swindon beat Chesterfield 3-0 this time, with Alan on the score-sheet.

QUITE A COMPARISON TO LIVE UP TO

When Andy King signed the French striker Eric Sabin in the summer of 2001 from Wasquehal he compared him to Thierry Henry. Although Sabin had Henry's pace and not dissimilar looks and stature he wasn't nearly as prolific. Sabin scored nine times in two seasons for the club before moving on to Queens Park Rangers. Sabin's career in England then took him on to Boston United, Northampton Town and Oxford United, where he was part of their squad relegated from the Football League, before he returned to his homeland.

THE MAD WORLD OF MILDENHALL

Swindon keeper Steve Mildenhall made his league debut for Town – as a striker! Mildenhall was thrown on up front late in a match at Tranmere Rovers in January 1997. Swindon were chasing the game at 2-1 down but it was one of Steve McMahon's more eccentric decisions. The Swindon-born player, who checks in at 6ft 4ins. tall, says he can't actually remember touching the ball. The keeper always seemed to be at the centre of things early on in his time at the club. He gave away a penalty on his full debut as a teenager in the League Cup at Cambridge United, while in his first league start at Portsmouth he needed stitches in his testicles after a nasty collision with Robbie Pethick. Mildenhall bravely went through the pain barrier to keep a clean sheet in a televised match that Swindon won 1-0 to move to the top of the First Division.

DON'T GO DIXON

Swindon fans made it pretty clear they didn't want Will Dixon to leave when he was given a free transfer in 1977 by clubbing together to get him a crystal pint mug to thank him for his service. A presentation was made to him after the news was made public. With the customary hair and outlandish moustache that dominated 1970s fashions, Dixon, signed from Colchester United, was a well respected figure at right-back and in central midfield, making 165 appearances over four seasons. To emphasise his popularity, he left the field to a standing ovation in his final match at home to Portsmouth.

SEVEN UP

Swindon have beaten one side 7-0 on two separate occasions – Aldershot. In September 1946 Bill Stephens scored four times in a Division Three (South) fixture at the County Ground, while the sides were paired in the FA Cup third round in the 1982/83 season with both teams in the Fourth Division. Andy Rowland and Howard Pritchard both got hat-tricks, with Paul Batty scoring the other goal to match the feat from 37 years previously.

FROM YOUR POCKET TO THE PITCH

Swindon fans have raised more than £30,000 to fund loan signings thanks to the Red Army Fund, an idea set up by TrustSTFC, the club's supporters trust. The most recent was defender Gordon Greer, who played an important part in preserving Swindon's League One status in 2008/09 before signing on a permanent basis. The others were Preston goalkeeper Andy Lonergan, the Brighton & Hove Albion striker Chris McPhee, and forward Michael Proctor. Proctor gave the fund a perfect start when he scored 25 minutes into his debut at the County Ground – it proved to be the winner against Port Vale on February 23rd 2005.

MAKING A BOW ON MATCH OF THE DAY

Swindon's first appearance on the BBC's *Match of the Day* came on April 13th 1968. In those days the programme would periodically cover games from the lower divisions and David Coleman and the cameras tuned up to capture Swindon's Division Three match with Southport, the Sandgrounders' first-ever visit to the County Ground. Before the game Coleman didn't sound too thrilled, saying: "This is one of the matches we cover each year from one of the lower divisions." He did perk up in the build-up though, focusing on Don Rogers, who is described as "the local idol" and "rated in the £100,000 class". It's also fascinating to see the County Ground before the new North Stand was built. Rogers lived up to his build up, scoring twice in a 3-3 draw including an injury time equaliser after Southport had counter-attacked their way into the lead. The final goal prompted a mini pitch invasion but Swindon ended the season in tenth place.

FLOWERS OF SCOTLAND

More than one hundred Scottish players have represented Swindon Town. This XI would be fun to put together and watch with some help from a nearby time machine, especially when it came to seeing any hapless striker trying to get through the defence. In Calderwood, Walker, Macari and Shearer it also includes four full Scottish internationals.

Jimmy Allan...................... goalkeeper 1971/83
Andy Cowie.......................right-back 1948/51
Colin Calderwood..... centre-back 1986/1993
Frank Burrows ....centre-back 1968/76
Jock Walker........................... left-back 1907/13
Willie Penman........... right-midfield 1966/69
Lou Macari.............. centre-midfield 1985/86
Ross MacLaren........ centre-midfield 1988/94
Jimmy Bain ....left-midfield 1947/54
Duncan Shearer...................... striker 1988/92
Chris Hay .... striker 1997/2000

LOVING THE LEAGUE CUP: PART THREE

Swindon's third trip to the League Cup semi-finals came under Steve McMahon in the 1994/95 season. The run was almost over before it began in the second round but Town overturned a 3-1 deficit against Charlton Athletic, winning 4-1 at the Valley thanks to a Jan Age Fjortoft hat-trick and a rare contribution from Joey Beauchamp, whose shot hit keeper Andy Petterson for an own goal. In the third round Swindon needed a replay to see off Second Division Brighton & Hove Albion after a 1-1 draw at the Goldstone – a game that saw defender Andy Thomson score his only goal for the club. The replay saw a comfortable 4-1 victory. Swindon edged past Derby County 2-1 in the fourth round with two more goals for Fjortoft. The quarter-final against Millwall saw a comfortable 3-1 win, and again Fjortoft struck to ensure he had scored in every round so far. A packed County Ground saw Swindon at home to Bolton Wanderers in the first semi-final, meaning they could make the final without facing a Premier League side. Peter Thorne's two goals gave Town a 2-1 lead to take to Burnden Park and Fjortoft's close range finish in the second leg made it 3-1 on aggregate.

Sadly, an under-strength Swindon couldn't hold on against the side going for promotion. Wanderers scored three times in the last half-hour and old nemesis John McGinlay completed the comeback with two minutes to go.

Round/Scorers	Opponents	Score
Second round First Leg	Charlton Athletic (H)	1-3
Scott		
Second round Second Leg	Charlton Athletic (A)	4-1
Fjortoft (3), Petterson (og)		
Third round	Brighton & Hove Albion (A)	1-1
Thomson		
Third round Replay	Brighton & Hove Albion (H)	4-1
Fjortoft (2), Scott (2)		
Fourth round	Derby County (H)	2-1
Fjortoft (2)		
Quarter Final	Millwall (H)	3-1
Mutch (2), Fjortoft		
Semi Final First Leg	Bolton Wanderers (H)	2-1
Thorne (2)		
Semi Final Second Leg	Bolton Wanderers (A)	1-3
Fjortoft		

DO YOU REALLY COME FROM A LAND DOWN UNDER?

Fans expecting Australian striker Dave Mitchell to have that familiar twang to his voice were always surprised the first time they heard him interviewed. Born in Glasgow but raised in Adelaide, Mitchell retained a broad Scottish accent despite moving to Australia at the age of six. It was only strengthened by a spell at Glasgow Rangers. The striker developed an effective partnership with Craig Maskell but left after two seasons to play in Turkey. He scored 24 goals in 80 games and his deceptive pace was missed up front. Mitchell has had a good coaching career since retiring, describing his Swindon boss Glenn Hoddle as his "coaching mentor". At the time of writing he is manager of Australian A-League side Perth Glory and has also given a presentation for the Australian Football Federation on goalscoring at a coaching conference.

HOME INTERNATIONALS

The following players have represented the four home nations and the Republic of Ireland during their time at Swindon Town. Rod Thomas, with thirty appearances for Wales, makes him the most capped Robin in club history. Jan Age Fjortoft (Norway), Ricky Shakes (Trinidad & Tobago) and Miguel Comminges (Guadeloupe) have all had international call-ups too.

England

Harold Fleming..................... 11 caps, 1909/14

Scotland

Jock Walker............................. 9 caps, 1911/13

Northern Ireland

Trevor Anderson................... 12 caps, 1975/78
Bryan Hamilton .... 7 caps, 1979/80
Kevin Horlock......................... 5 caps, 1995/97
Jimmy Quinn................................. 6 caps, 1988
Norman Uprichard................. 5 caps, 1952/53

Wales

Paul Bodin .... 17 caps, 1990 & 1992/94
Rod Thomas........................... 30 caps, 1967/74

Republic of Ireland

Tony Galvin .... 1 cap, 1990
Alan McLoughlin .... 5 caps, 1990/91
Ray Treacy............................. 11 caps, 1972/74

UNDER-21s

Swindon's County Ground has staged three England under-21 internationals. There have been two friendlies, a 3-0 win over Romania in 1981 and a 1-1 draw with Switzerland in 1996, plus one European Championship qualifier. England drew 1-1 with Italy on April 23rd 1986. Two Town players have been picked for the under-21s during their time with the club. They are goalkeeper Fraser Digby and winger Nicky Summerbee.

WHEN I'M SIXTY FOUR (GAMES INTO A SEASON)

Swindon played a remarkable 64 games in the 1986/87 season. It all began on August 23rd 1986 with a win at Bolton Wanderers in the first of 46 regulation Football League matches in Division Three. There were four more games in the early rounds of the Littlewoods Cup, four in the FA Cup, plus another five in the Freight Rover Trophy and finally five in the play-offs, with the two-legged semi-finals and final, plus the decisive final match with Gillingham at Selhurst Park that ended it all on May 29th 1987.

ANOTHER BLACK DAY FOR BOBBY

Ten years after Bobby Moore was beaten at Swindon in an FA Cup replay with West Ham United, he found himself back at the County Ground with Fulham in the 1976/77 season. It was the era when Moore, George Best and Rodney Marsh were turning out for the London side. Swindon, who had drawn 3-3 at Craven Cottage, demolished their big name opponents 5-0 in the third round replay, where the famous names were swept aside by two goals each from Dave Syrett and Dave Moss, plus one from Trevor Anderson.

KINDNESS TO KEEPERS

Swindon tried to pioneer the introduction of substitute goalkeepers back in 1965. At the end of the season they led a proposal to the Football Association to allow a substitute keeper on at any time if the referee agreed the goalie was not fit enough to continue to play. Manchester United seconded the idea, but it failed to go through. In the first game of the 1964/65 season Town keeper Norman Oakley suffered a shoulder injury right at the start of the game. They were beaten 6-1 at Bury with Owen Dawson replacing Oakley. Swindon ended up being relegated by one point.

COMMERCIALLY MINDED

Sporting stars and endorsements are thought of as a pretty modern thing, but Swindon's Maurice Owen was among the early trendsetters. As early as 1951 striker Owen was telling fans through adverts in the local press that Quaker Oats is "my food for action", with the advert claiming that it gave him "match-winning fitness".

THE ULTIMATE ONE CLUB SERVANT

John Trollope MBE is etched through the history of Swindon Town from the 1960s to the present day and holds the record for most league appearances for one club, one which seems destined never to be beaten. The left-back, from Wroughton, was given his first team debut on the opening day of the 1960/61 season by manager Bert Head after impressing in pre-season. He was just 17-years-old. From then on he was to become a fixture in Swindon teams for close-on twenty years as an attacking full-back who seemed to form an instinctive understanding with another Swindon youth team graduate, Don Rogers. After a brief spell on the sidelines in Easter 1961, thanks to a stomach muscle strain, Trollope would go on to play 368 consecutive league matches. He helped Swindon to a first Football League promotion in 1962/63 and even played a game up front, at Oldham in 1966, before being sidelined by a broken arm at Hartlepool in August 1968. Trollope had to battle to reclaim his place in the side when he was back fit but by the time the 1969 League Cup final came around he was in the left-back berth to be part of the side that saw off Arsenal. Trollope was pretty much dropped just once in his Swindon career. It came under Les Allen as Swindon's decline and descent into Division Three gathered pace. In January 1974 he overtook Maurice Owen's club appearance record. The pair had played together when Trollope was breaking into the side and Owen had dropped back into defence. In 1978 he announced his retirement, aged 34, after 738 league games to become youth team coach, though he was clearly capable of continuing to play at first team level. His loyalty saw him nominated for an MBE, which he received from the Queen in November 1978. Retirement didn't last long. Two months into the 1978/79 season he was asked to fill in at right-back and he ended the campaign just nine games short of the Portsmouth legend Jimmy Dickinson's one-club appearance record as Swindon narrowly missed out on promotion. Again though his career looked over, as Swindon brought in John Templeman to play at full-back and Trollope focused on his work with the next generation of Swindon players. In 1980/81 Swindon made a terrible start to the season, losing the opening five matches. Manager Bobby Smith asked a shocked Trollope, then 37, to come back into defence to replace one of his big money signings, David Peach.

There was also a minor culture shock for Trollope on his return – he was actually being part of a warm-up before a game! Smith was sacked fairly soon afterwards. It saw general manager Danny Williams back in caretaker charge and he kept faith with the full-back who had served him so well. It meant that on October 18th 1980, Trollope made league appearance 765, breaking Dickinson's record, in a 1-1 draw with Carlisle United at the County Ground. He was able to keep Peter Beardsley quiet in the process. Trollope only stopped playing in November 1980 to take over as manager, finishing with 770 league appearances and 889 first team games for Swindon Town, which remains as the record as the most appearances for one club. Trollope's spell as boss was less successful and he has described agreeing to take the job as his "worst decision in football". With little money to spend, good players like Alan Mayes sold off, and no real cash to pay decent wages, let alone transfer fees, Trollope found life difficult in Division Three. Swindon narrowly survived in 1980/81, and he was unable to prevent Swindon falling into Division Four for the first time in 1982. With promotion hopes fading away in the following season he was sacked as manager in March 1983, returning immediately to his youth team manager's position with a sense of relief as well as disappointment. Some of the players Trollope signed, notably Jimmy Quinn from Oswestry for £2,000 and a set of kit, and Leigh Barnard went on to be part of happier eras. In Easter 1985 he was back working with the first team. Trollope was asked by Lou Macari to be his assistant after the departure of Harry Gregg. He stayed in that role as Town won back-to-back promotions before again fulfilling the youth team coaching role following the arrival of former Swindon striker Chic Bates as Macari's assistant. The unfortunate Trollope eventually found himself in the witness box as part of the illegal payments scandal of 1990 and subsequent tax trial. He remained with the club until his abrupt dismissal by Steve McMahon in 1996 after 37 years' service. It seemed a sudden and disrespectful end to his time with Swindon. After his departure he worked as a postman, with the Bristol Rovers youth set up, the Football League and Wolverhampton Wanderers before, in a move to delight Town fans, it was announced he was coming back to Swindon in the summer of 2008 to coach at the Centre of Excellence.

PUTTING CITY IN THEIR PLACE

The last game of the 1986/87 season didn't matter in one sense, as Swindon were already safely in the play-offs. In another sense, it couldn't have mattered more. Firstly, it was a local derby at Bristol City and secondly, City needed a win to join Swindon in the play-offs and have a chance of promotion into Division Two. In front of a gate of more than 19,000, Trevor Morgan headed City in front from a free kick… but Peter Coyne volleyed in an equaliser in the second half to bring joy to the Town support. City then won a controversial penalty. Tim Parkin was adjudged to have impeded Joe Jordan in a scramble for the ball but Gordon Owen rolled the spot kick wide of Digby's right-hand post and Swindon held out for a very sweet point. Bristolian tempers boiled over during the game as they banged on the roof of the Swindon dug-out while, in a pitch invasion that followed the final whistle, Dave Bamber was knocked to the ground by two City fans.

IT FELT A LONG, LONG TIME

Swindon's longest barren Football League run without a goal stretched 518 minutes. It came in the first season in Division Two in 1962/63. After Ernie Hunt netted at Middlesbrough there were five straight shut outs against Newcastle United, Huddersfield Town, Derby County, Swansea Town and Scunthorpe United, before Hunt ended the sequence with a goal at home to Portsmouth after more than a month's wait. Oddly enough, though, Town found the net three times against Division One West Ham United in the League Cup during that barren league sequence.

DAMN THAT DEAN

On the last day of the 2006/07 season Swindon were denied victory in their final game of the season against Walsall, though they still clinched promotion, when Dean Keates thumped an injury time free kick past Phil Smith to make it 1-1. On the final day of the 2008/09 season, Swindon were at promoted Peterborough United and leading 2-1 in injury time only for the Posh to get a free kick, which was driven home by – yes, Dean Keates – to make the score 2-2 and rob Town of three points again.

THE ETERNAL WAIT FOR A WIN

With Swindon's financial problems gradually worsening and fans driven away by the unloved Steve McMahon era, Jimmy Quinn was given a mighty difficult inheritance as manager. In his first season in 1998/99 Quinn did well to keep Swindon in Division One. In 1999/2000 though, the wheels finally came off despite Quinn's best efforts, leading to the club's longest sequence of Football League games without a win. A 2-0 defeat at Bolton Wanderers on October 30th 1999 was the start of a club-record 19-match run without a league victory that went through Christmas and New Year and eventually into March. Finally, on March 7th 2000, Huddersfield Town were beaten 2-0 at home, with Lee Collins' goal and Chris Hay's penalty providing much relief. The crowd of 4,701 for a second tier fixture indicates how bad the decline had become. Just to be perverse, the side won their next game as well, a 1-0 victory at the eventual league winners Charlton Athletic.

FIREWORK MAN SAM

Keeper Sam Burton played in goal for Swindon in three different decades, the 1940s, 1950s and 60s. The long-serving player also acquired a reputation as one of the team's practical jokers. In Peter Matthews' excellent biography of John Trollope, *John Trollope – Record Breaker,* the Town full-back tells the story of one of Burton's escapades. With the players changing in the Shrivenham Road pavilion, Burton managed to get a firework through an outside vent, into a toilet cubicle, hitting one of the pans and exploding... a pan where the youthful Ernie Hunt was busy in action! Hunt thankfully emerged intact.

SUPREME FROM THE SPOT

On April 24th 1976, Swindon were facing Walsall at home and were still not quite sure of securing Third Division status for another season. Then came a virtuoso performance of penalty taking from Northern Ireland international Trevor Anderson. Referee Lester Shapter awarded three spot kicks against the Saddlers – and four in the match overall. After Walsall went in front, Anderson came to the fore. He put the first past keeper Mick Kearns to the right, went the other way for the second and, for variety, stuck the third into the roof of the net. Swindon went on to win 5-1.

THE PROMOTION SEASON THAT NEVER WAS – 1989/90

While promotion was ultimately taken away, the on-pitch success of 1990 remains worth recording, with the side finishing in a then highest-ever league placing of fourth in Division Two. Ossie Ardiles came in to replace Lou Macari as manager after he left for West Ham United. Ardiles produced a side where the focus was more on passing and possession than the high tempo, fitness-based game Macari had demanded. Ardiles played a diamond formation with Alan McLoughlin allowed an attack-minded free role which he revelled in. A slow start saw one win in the opening seven matches, but a 3-0 win at home to Plymouth Argyle got things going, while Stoke City were swept aside 6-0 in November. Ardiles also made an astute purchase in David Kerslake from Queens Park Rangers, with left-back Phil King heading to Sheffield Wednesday. Perhaps the highlight came in February, where Ardiles' side came from a goal down to beat the eventual champions Leeds United 3-2, with a wonderful drive from Ross MacLaren. As the *Sunday People* kept pumping out its revelations about betting and payments to players, the squad and Ardiles showed admirable resolve when it came to on-pitch matters and while it always looked difficult to catch Leeds, automatic promotion was in reach going into the last ten games of the season. In the end though, a fourth-place finish saw a play-off semi-final with Blackburn Rovers. Steve White opened the scoring at Ewood Park, before a sensational Steve Foley volley, as clean a strike as you can imagine, made it 2-0. Rovers pulled it back to 2-1, but the same score-line at the County Ground saw Swindon heading back to Wembley. Duncan Shearer's clever lob made it 3-1 on aggregate, just crossing the line, before another Steve White goal made it 2-0 on the night. A late Blackburn deflection made no difference. The play-off final at Wembley saw a meeting with Sunderland, who had knocked local rivals Newcastle United out in the other semi. Almost 73,000 gathered at Wembley and saw Swindon win just 1-0, which appeared to be the biggest injustice on the day. Alan McLoughlin's deflected shot was the only goal, but Swindon created by far the better and more numerous chances. The promotion celebrations though, were soon cut short by the Football League. Duncan Shearer and Steve White finished as joint top-scorers, each getting 27 goals, with Alan McLoughlin scoring 17 times from midfield.

1990 PROMOTION CELEBRATIONS: SOON CUT SHORT

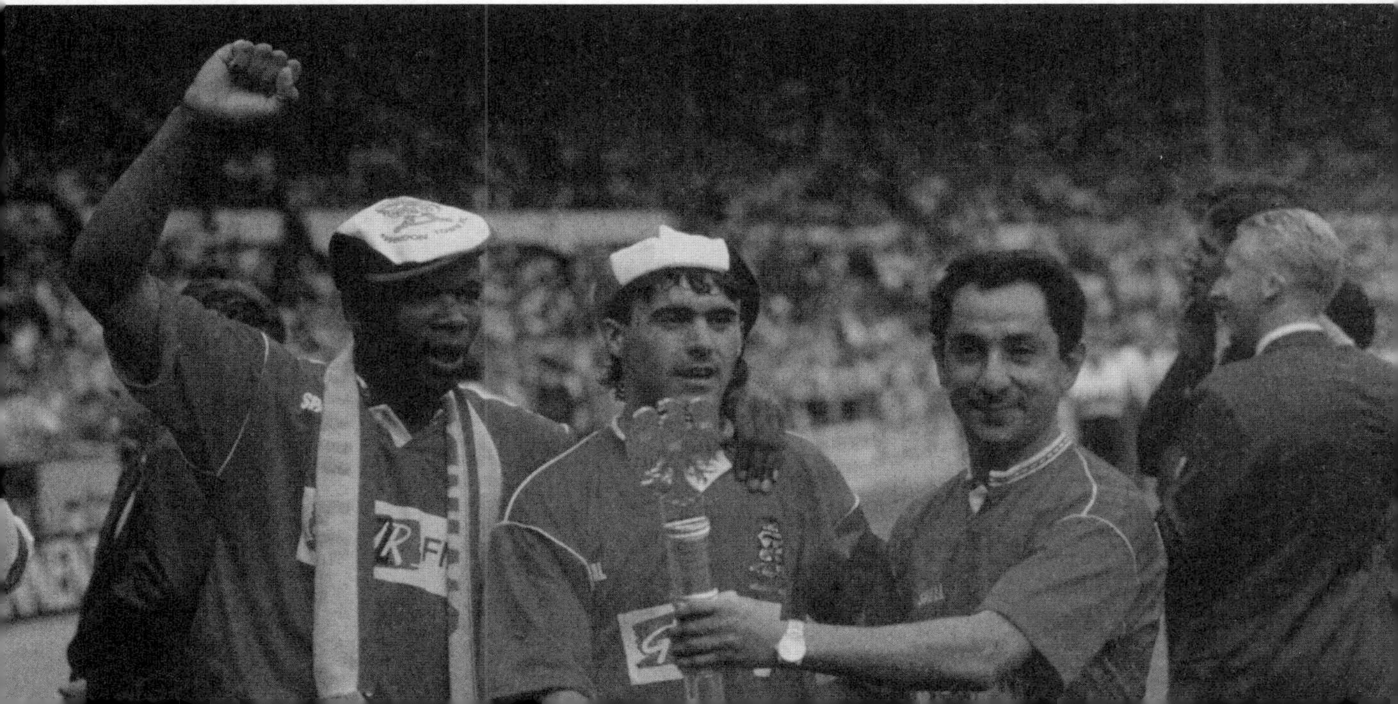

FIRST DIVISION FOOTBALL FOR TEN DAYS

On May 28th 1990 Swindon appeared to have finally won promotion into the top flight for the first time after winning that Division Two play-off final at Wembley against Sunderland. There was also a caveat, in that they were waiting to find out the punishment for admitting 36 charges of illegal payments over five years. The Football League delayed its hearing until after the play-offs. On June 7th 1990 came the verdict. Don Rogers had delivered a 44,000-signature petition to the league's management committee ahead of the meeting. The hearing, at Villa Park, lasted eight hours. The announcement eventually came from David Dent, the Football League secretary. After outlining the details he gave news of the savage punishment in Part Four of his statement. "Swindon Town Football Club be demoted by two divisions – i.e. to the Third Division for season 1990/91". Chairman Gary Herbert could merely sum up his reaction as "devastating" before leaving a press conference. Fans gathered at the County Ground not only in anger at the punishment, but at being parted with their money to watch a league campaign and a Wembley final that meant nothing. Around 20,000 fans staged a protest march through the streets and Swindon had a High Court hearing to see if they could pursue legal action. Eventually the case went to an FA appeal and after five hours of hearing the arguments, the punishment was halved. Promotion was still wiped out but there was at least a place in Division Two. Years on the case of Boston United had similar echoes, after the club won the Conference but was found guilty of illegal payments. Their punishment – a fine and a four-point deduction, but their promotion was kept intact and they had a first ever experience of the Football League.

STRENGTH BEYOND MERE MORTALS

Swindon's long-serving centre-back George Hudson, who was with the club throughout the 1950s, is often described as a real giant of a man. His physique was so impressive he got the nickname Garth, after the hero from the *Daily Mirror* comic strips. Garth had super-human powers of strength and would battle villains from across different eras in time. George just had the ability to keep centre-forwards quiet in more than 400 games for the club.

NO VALE OF TEARS

In 2003/04 Swindon were in contention for the play-offs when they visited Port Vale, who also had promotion hopes, at the end of March. The game was delayed by floodlight failure and Swindon didn't get going till even later with Town 3-0 behind after an hour. In the last thirty minutes, though, Swindon had Rory Fallon, Sam Parkin and Tommy Mooney all on up front and started hitting the ball long to the physical Fallon. The game changed totally. Parkin headed in the first goal from Andy Nicholas' cross. Then, you could sense the momentum shift when, five minutes later, Matt Hewlett scored with Vale struggling to clear their lines. Swindon had 22 minutes left to find an equaliser and battered the home side. Finally, with just seven minutes left, Parkin got to the by-line and his cross was chested home by Rory Fallon in front of the travelling fans to make it 3-3. It was a fantastic turnaround in its own right but the true significance comes when you see the league table at the end of the season.

Division Two Final Table

	P	W	D	L	GF	GA	PTS	GD
5. Swindon Town (POs)	46	20	13	13	76	58	73	+18
6. Hartlepool (POs)	46	20	13	13	76	61	73	+15
7. Port Vale	46	21	10	15	73	63	73	+10

FROM KEEPING TO COMEDY

Scottish goalkeeping is traditionally a soft target to lampoon, so Swindon goalkeeper Frank Haffey decided to turn self-parody into part of his new career. He was signed from Celtic in 1964 as Town struggled in Division Two following the injury to first choice Norman Oakley. Haffey was infamous as the man who played in goal for Scotland in a 9-3 defeat at Wembley three years earlier. Haffey made just four appearances before a fall out with manager Bert Head. He ended up emigrating to Australia and carved out a career as a nightclub entertainer with an act of singing and comedy, some of it based on his goalkeeping experiences. He also appeared in a cult Australian World War II TV drama *Spyforce* as an extra, as did a future star called Russell Crowe.

"IT'S THE SHOT OF THE SEASON"

If a Swindon goal was good enough to get HTV's Roger Malone excited, you could be guaranteed it was pretty special. Kenny Stroud's equaliser against Everton in the FA Cup in 1977 fell into that category – it won the Central TV Goal of the Season. With fans paying extra to get in – prices for seats shot up from £1 to £1.50 and standing from 65p to £1 – Swindon were twice behind in the game. Dave Syrett had pounced on Ray McHale's blocked shot after Duncan McKenzie gave Everton the lead. Bob Latchford then made it 2-1 for Everton with a well worked corner but then came Stroud's moment of national prominence. On a pitch coated in sand he picked up the ball about 35 yards out in a central position and his right-foot shot whistled in off the post in front of the Town End to level the scores. Stroud's superb strike earned Swindon a replay at Goodison Park, where Trevor Anderson gave Town the lead with eleven minutes to go before Everton scored twice. A certain Andy King was in the Everton midfield for both games.

ADMINISTRATION

In the chaotic spell at the start of the millennium, Swindon were the first club in the country to go into administration twice. The first time came in January 2000 with the club losing a reported £25,000 a week. Chairman Rikki Hunt resigned, 15 staff lost their jobs and an exodus of players followed, including striker Chris Hay leaving for just £75,000. Eventually, a deal was done with the creditors, but in March 2002, with many clubs suffering after the collapse of ITV Digital, the club couldn't pay its phone bill, while the PFA was paying the players' wages. At one point in March director Bob Holt even told manager Andy King the club was going under the following day.

NO ID FOR ME

Swindon fans were among those protesting at Conservative plans for ID cards for supporters put forward by Margaret Thatcher's government in 1989. A petition of more than 2,000 signatures was delivered to the local Tory MP Simon Coombs by Town supporters.

THEY CAME, THEY SAW, THEY SCORED

Swindon's top league scorers since 1960:

1960/61	Ernie Hunt	14	Division Three
1961/62	Ernie Hunt	18	Division Three
1962/63	Ernie Hunt	24	Division Three
1963/64	Ernie Hunt	12	Division Two
1964/65	Mike Summerbee	13	Division Two
1965/66	Keith East & Don Rogers	19	Division Three
1966/67	Don Rogers	24	Division Three
1967/68	Don Rogers	25	Division Three
1968/69	Don Rogers	22	Division Three
1969/70	Arthur Horsfield	18	Division Two
1970/71	Don Rogers	16	Division Two
1971/72	Peter Noble	14	Division Two
1972/73	Ray Treacy	13	Division Two
1973/74	Peter Eastoe	8	Division Two
1974/75	Peter Eastoe	26	Division Three
1975/76	Trevor Anderson	15	Division Three
1976/77	Trevor Anderson & David Moss	14	Division Three
1977/78	David Moss	16	Division Three
1978/79	Chic Bates	14	Division Three
1979/80	Andy Rowland	20	Division Three
1980/81	Andy Rowland	12	Division Three
1981/82	Paul Rideout	14	Division Three
1982/83	Paul Rideout	20	Division Four
1983/84	Alan Mayes	17	Division Four
1984/85	Colin Gordon	17	Division Four
1985/86	Charlie Henry	18	Division Four
1986/87	Steve White	17	Division Three
1987/88	Jimmy Quinn	21	Division Two
1988/89	Duncan Shearer	14	Division Two
1989/90	Duncan Shearer	21	Division Two
1990/91	Duncan Shearer	22	Division Two
1991/92	Duncan Shearer	22	Division Two
1992/93	Craig Maskell	21	Division One
1993/94	Jan Age Fjortoft	12	Premier League

1994/95	Jan Age Fjortoft	15	Division One
1995/96	Wayne Allison	17	Division Two
1996/97	Wayne Allison	11	Division One
1997/98	Chris Hay	14	Division One
1998/99	Iffy Onuora	20	Division One
1999/00	Chris Hay	10	Division One
2000/01	Danny Invincible	9	Division Two
2001/02	Giuliano Grazioli	8	Division Two
2002/03	Sam Parkin	25	Division Two
2003/04	Sam Parkin	20	Division Two
2004/05	Sam Parkin	23	League One
2005/06	Rory Fallon	12	League One
2006/07	Christian Roberts & Lee Peacock	10	League Two
2007/08	Simon Cox	15	League One
2008/09	Simon Cox	29	League One

START AS YOU MEAN TO GO ON

Four players have scored hat-tricks on their Swindon debuts since the club entered the Football League and all went on to have prolific Swindon careers. The first, not surprisingly, is all-time record scorer Harry Morris. The second was Maurice Owen in January 1947 against Watford, and he went on to net more than 100 Swindon goals. The third was Alan Mayes, who was signed from Watford for £80,000 in February 1979. Mayes got all three goals on his debut in a 3-1 win over Rotherham United at Millmoor. The fourth is Sam Parkin, who started life off in a Swindon shirt with his hat-trick in a 3-1 win over Barnsley on the opening day of the 2002/03 season, getting his third and final goal with a late penalty.

LETTER FROM SOUTH AMERICA

Swindon went on a tour of South America back in 1912, playing in Argentina and Uruguay – and returned unbeaten, with six wins and two draws, including a match against a representative Argentinian XI which drew more than twenty thousand fans. Swindon secretary-manager Sam Allen was impressed, telling one newspaper: "The standard of play was much higher than we had been led to expect... many of the men who played in the more important teams could easily earn a living in England as professionals."

DEBUT DOUBLE

Not too much was known about Slovakian keeper Peter Brezovan when Dennis Wise brought him to the County Ground, but his impact was immediate. Brezovan stood an impressive 6ft 6ins. tall and his giant presence clearly helped as he saved two penalties on his debut at Hartlepool on August 5th 2006. Brezovan was just three minutes into his Swindon career when he dived low to his right to stop Joel Porter's spot kick, blocking the follow up superbly. Then, in the second half, he went the other way to keep out Ritchie Humphreys' penalty and get Swindon off to a winning start in their promotion season. Brezovan, who broke his arm later that season in a game with Grimsby Town, never looked quite the same on his return and was released at the end of the 2008/9 season.

JUSTICE DONE, JUST FOUR MONTHS ON

Perhaps Swindon's best performance of the 1976/77 league season has been wiped out from the record books. On New Year's Day 1977 Town were at home to a Brighton & Hove Albion side who went on to win promotion. After the pitch had passed a number of early inspections, Danny Williams' side ripped into their opponents, and with 67 minutes gone they were leading 4-0 thanks to a Kenny Stroud special, plus a goal from Dave Syrett and two strikes from Ray McHale. Midway through the second half, enter some sleet – enough to prompt referee Alan Robinson to call a halt to proceedings, insisting the pitch had turned things into a farce. Even the Brighton manager Alan Mullery admitted it was a huge slice of luck. The game was finally re-arranged for May, with a different referee. Swindon, who were in dismal form, came through 2-1 after falling behind early, with Ray McHale getting one of his missing goals back by scoring with a free kick .

PETER AND HIS PIGEONS

League Cup-winning keeper Peter Downsborough's big relaxation away from football was keeping and racing homing pigeons. His birds were clearly well looked after and well trained. In 1970 Downsborough – and pigeons – won the McIlroy Cup, one of six trophies presented by the Stratton and District Homing Society.

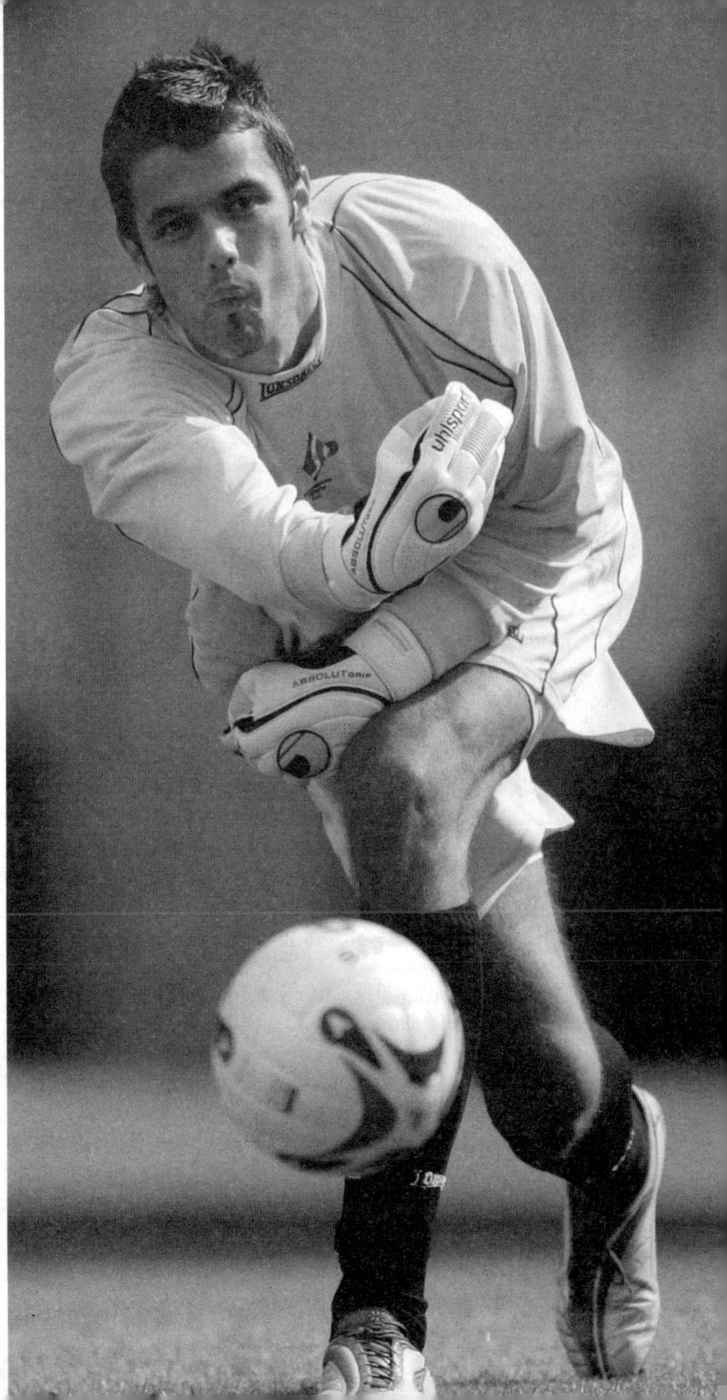

PETER BREZOVAN: A GOOD ARTIST WHEN NOT SAVING SPOT KICKS

ONE PHONE CALL TELLS ALL

Swindon players found out they had been relegated from Division Two at the end of the 1964/65 thanks to a phone call made in the middle of Andover. Bert Head's squad were travelling back home after a final day defeat at Southampton. Portsmouth had started the day in the bottom two and they played in the evening at promoted Northampton Town with the significant advantage of knowing they now just needed a point to stay up. The kick-off time had been changed by the Cobblers, who wanted to try an evening kick-off to improve gates. The league were happy to allow this despite the obvious advantage given to Pompey. Portsmouth drew 1-1, Swindon were back in Division Three after two seasons and Bert Head lost his job.

Division Two Final Table

	P	W	D	L	GF	GA	PTS	AV
20. Portsmouth	42	12	10	20	56	77	34	0.73
21. Swindon Town (R)	42	14	5	23	63	81	33	0.98
22. Swansea Town (R)	42	11	10	21	62	84	32	0.74

FOR THE BEST?

Swindon came very close to going into overseas ownership in 2007 in a bizarre takeover saga that rumbled on for almost four months. It began in July when BEST holdings were gradually revealed as the company interested. It took a while to establish exactly who they were. Various public faces were Rufus Brevett, a former Oxford and Queens Park Rangers defender who arrived with the title of sporting director, then American chairman designate Jim Little appeared. Eventually, more of a clue seemed to arrive with Portugese agent Jose Veiga's involvement as he was named general manager and appeared on the pitch ahead of a home game with Yeovil Town. Despite appointments, announcements and the apparent purchase of players – the sudden appearance of Portugese defender Mauro Almeida in a Johnstone's Paint Trophy match took many by surprise – the deal finally fell apart in October despite announcements by the owners that everything was in the final stages and just "tiny points" needed to be ironed out. Both sides blamed each other.

ST. ANDREW'S MIRACLE

The king of Swindon comebacks was an Easter resurrection. On April 12th 1993, Easter Monday, Swindon trailed Birmingham City 4-1 at St. Andrew's with almost an hour gone. Then there were five unanswered goals in half an hour. Craig Maskell began things when he made it 4-2, then Dave Mitchell scored with a diving header. At 4-3 the momentum was irresistible. With 14 minutes to go Maskell and Mitchell teamed up to make it 4-4. Swindon took the lead for the first time when Maskell looped in a header from a corner to complete a four-goal spree in 18 remarkable minutes. Australian Mitchell then rounded the keeper at the death to make it 6-4, leaving Andy Gosney sprawling in wholly appropriate fashion in a seven-goal second half.

DON'T FERRY ME ACROSS THE MERSEY...

Swindon sponsors Lowndes Lambert wanted a high profile name to replace manager Ken Beamish in 1984 in return for their investment. Initially, the club interviewed some experienced bosses, among them Alan Durban, former Swindon player Bryan Hamilton and Gordon Lee, before the sponsor decided the club had to hire a big name player-manager instead. It turned out to be the start of the Macari era, but despite his achievements he wasn't first choice. Liverpool defender Phil Thompson, who won seven championships while at Anfield, was twice interviewed by the Swindon board, but eventually decided life in Division Four was not for him. The board then turned to Macari, who had been one of their early candidates, along with Kenny Hibbitt.

OLD ENOUGH TO SCORE, JUST NOT TO VOTE

Striker Paul Rideout is the youngest Swindon player to score a goal. Rideout, an England schoolboy international, was given his debut by manager John Trollope in a home game with Hull City on November 29th 1980, aged 16 years and 107 days. Not only did he score in a 3-1 win at the County Ground but he also had another goal disallowed. His performances were one of the few bright spots in Swindon's bleak period in the early 1980s. Two other 16-year-olds have scored in Swindon colours; Ernie Hunt and Andy Caton.

DIVISION OF LABOUR

When Swindon kicked off the 2009/10 season it was their 29th campaign in the third tier of the Football League. Using the old divisions One to Four, here's how long Swindon have spent in each.

Division One 1
Division Two...18
Division Three..29
Division Three (South)..................................31
Division Four...5

COURTING TROUBLE

Chris Kamara's two spells at Swindon were mostly happy ones; being part of the 1979 League Cup run and returning for a second spell to help begin the climb out of the Football League basement in 1985. His last game, though, produced a sorry sporting first. In February 1988 Swindon were playing Shrewsbury Town at Gay Meadow. In an act completely out of character, Kamara elbowed the Shrews striker Jim Melrose as the players left the pitch, leaving him with a fractured cheekbone. The club quickly suspended Kamara for a month and fined him £1,000, a course of action he accepted. The case later went to court and Kamara was found guilty of GBH, the first player to be convicted in the courts over an on-field incident. Kamara was fined £1,200 this time and also ordered to pay compensation of £250. The game at Shrewsbury proved to be the last of Kamara's Swindon career, which should really have finished on a happier note. He signed for Stoke that summer.

HOME & AWAY

Swindon have twice been drawn away to non-league opponents in the FA Cup only to have games switched back to the County Ground. In November 1981, Swindon had to come from behind to beat Taunton 2-1 in a game that was officially an away tie, but the Somerset club opted for a switch for financial reasons. Five years later, the same thing happened when Swindon's scheduled game at Farnborough was switched from Cherrywood Road to Wiltshire, with the 2,000-capacity ground that lacked turnstiles not deemed suitable. This time Swindon won 4-0.

GOING UP: PART FOUR 1992/93

In 1991/92 Swindon had just missed out on the play-offs under Glenn Hoddle following the sale of Duncan Shearer. So, for the start of the 1992/93 season getting in a striker was crucial. Craig Maskell was his choice arriving from Reading in a swap deal with Tom Jones. Maskell quickly settled into goalscoring form and it was soon clear another play-off challenge was on. Notts County were routed 5-1 at home and a goalless draw at champions-elect Newcastle on national TV brought widespread praise for both sides for the quality of their football. Defender Shaun Taylor proved impossible for opponents to contain from set pieces, scoring 13 times in all. The chant of "Ooh, Shaun Taylor" would rise up before just about any corner. February and March brought some excellent results – full-back Paul Bodin just kept scoring. He netted in a 3-0 win over Millwall, while Steve White fired a hat-trick in a 4-0 victory over Watford. Champions Newcastle were beaten at home, but the top two were never quite in reach and there was the customary player sale late in the season when full-back David Kerslake went to Leeds United. Easter Monday saw the epic comeback over Birmingham City and Town ended up facing Tranmere in the play-offs. Steve Vickers was Swindon's extra man as Glenn Hoddle's team grabbed the tie by the throat in the first leg. Vickers headed in an own goal and gave the ball away for number two as Town sprinted into a three-goal lead. The game finished 3-1 and Swindon came through the second leg at Prenton Park, although Tranmere reduced the deficit to one goal, Craig Maskell gave Town breathing space and despite a late penalty Swindon were back to Wembley, with a chance to win promotion and slay the ghost of 1990. Swindon went 3-0 up as Hoddle passed a shot into the net, Maskell's effort made a gloriously satisfying thud off the post and Shaun Taylor scrambled in a third. Alan Parry's commentary at the time goes: "That surely means it's the Premier League for Swindon Town now." Chicken counting anyone? Leicester rattled in three goals in thirteen minutes to level the tie. Then though, everyone seemed to take a collective pause for breath, Swindon regrouped and brought on Steve White, a 1990 survivor. Late on, he chased Hoddle's long ball, carrying on into the penalty area, where keeper Kevin Poole and White collided. David Elleray decided penalty. Paul Bodin, who normally placed his penalties high into the net, rolled the ball past Poole and somehow the remaining minutes went past, to finally ensure Swindon would have top flight football. On reflection, the sad thing is the team that got there broke up immediately, with the departures of Glenn Hoddle and Colin Calderwood. As the years go by, the achievement seems more and more remarkable.

Division One Final Table

	P	W	D	L	GF	GA	PTS
1. Newcastle United (C)	46	29	9	8	92	38	96
2. West Ham United (P)	46	26	10	10	81	41	88
3. Portsmouth	46	26	10	10	80	46	88
4. Tranmere Rovers	46	23	10	13	72	56	79
5. Swindon Town (P)	46	21	13	12	74	59	76
6. Leicester City	46	22	10	14	71	64	76

SUPREME SHOT STOPPERS

This is the top ten of Swindon keepers, in terms of numbers of clean sheets. Peter Downsborough is the only one in this list to have an average of better than one clean sheet per three games played, though Len Skiller deserves note for his record when playing in the pre-war days when goals were easier to come by.

Fraser Digby .... 145 in 505 games 1986/98
Sam Burton .... 123 in 509 games 1945/61
Peter Downsborough .... 112 in 320 games 1965/73
Jimmy Allan .... 111 in 436 games 1971/83
Len Skiller .... 104 in 333 games 1909/22
Ted Nash .... 60 in 253 games 1920/30
Archie Ling .... 50 in 163 games 1905/09
Fred Hemmings .... 34 in 109 games 1902/12
Rhys Evans .... 32 in 128 games 2003/06
Scott Endersby .... 31 in 100 games 1983/85

LOWERING THE BAR

Fans attending games before the Second World War who arrived early would sometimes get to see Swindon playing their games in the English Schoolboys under-14 competition. The youngsters played on a full-size pitch, but a special crossbar was put in place to lower the height of the goals.

WHITE OR RED IT DOESN'T MATTER

Swindon fans have an enduring fondness for striker Steve White for his plentiful goals, pulled up shorts, high work-rate and curiously elbow laden style during some of the most successful days in club history. He scored more than a hundred goals in his time at the club and did that rarest of things for an away forward when he won a penalty at Old Trafford against Manchester United. This affection manifested itself on his return to the County Ground with Hereford United in the Auto Windscreens Shield on November 29th 1995. Just on half-time, White pounced to score from close range and while the Hereford fans cheered, the rest of the ground soon broke out into a spontaneous round of applause that left only manager Steve McMahon bemused.

WHAT DID WE START?

The formation of the Premier League has changed football beyond recognition. You can have your own argument whether it has been for the game's betterment or not, but the former FA chief executive Graham Kelly has stated that Swindon, inadvertently, are a big part of how it all began. He believes the Football Association's decision, after appeal, to reinstate Swindon back into Division Two in 1990 caused massive bad blood between the FA and the Football League. The League's initial punishment, of course, was to stick Town into Division Three. Kelly has said: "It is no exaggeration to state that deep in the roots of such acrimony lay the formation of the FA Premier League."

PREPARE TO PRAY, ITS PENALTIES

Swindon have a poor record over the last decade in penalty shoot-outs, having lost four of the last five they have been involved with. There was a marathon 7-6 win at Aldershot in the Johnstone's Paint Trophy that put an end a sequence which saw pain at Barnet in the FA Cup, at home to Brentford in the Carling Cup, at Brighton in the play-offs and a spot kick defeat in a Carling Cup match with Leeds United. The overall record stands at four successes out of nine though, with the first ever competitive shoot-out against Torquay United at Plainmoor in the Freight Rover Trophy in February 1985.

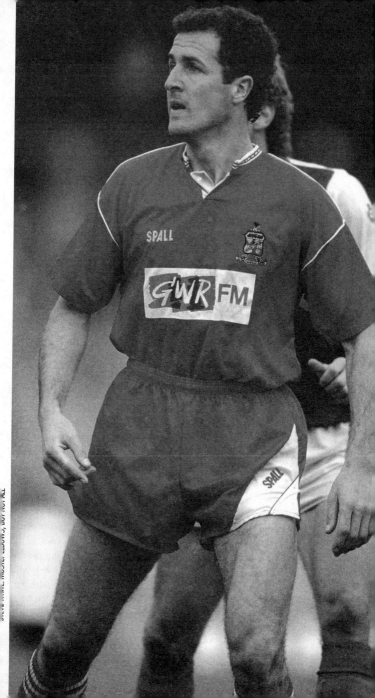

THE SAD TALE OF THE TAX TRIAL

The illegal payments that cost Swindon promotion in 1990 ultimately ended up in the law courts in the summer of 1992. The trial of former chairman Brian Hillier, manager Lou Macari and club accountant Vince Farrar went on for five weeks, with the court sitting for 26 days. It saw former players give evidence. Among them were Paul Bodin, who discussed what happened to his signing-on fee when he joined from Newport County. John Trollope was also called on to give evidence. When the jury gave their verdicts they agreed with Lou Macari that he had no part to play in matters of tax, saying players needed help with high property costs and that they were entitled to share financially in the bigger gates that came with success. Macari was acquitted. Hillier and Farrar, however, were found guilty, with the judge Ian Starforth-Hill saying football needed cleaning up. In his sentencing he said: "It is high time someone was made an example of to make sure this doesn't happen again." Farrar was given a suspended sentence, but Hillier was handed a prison term. The estimate was around £100,000 worth of tax was owed, which was repaid.

THE ETERNAL CUP TIE

Swindon's third round Littlewoods Cup tie with Bolton Wanderers in 1989 took almost a month to complete. It involved more than seven-and-a-half hours of football and unless the rules change, will be the longest running tie ever in the competition. The odyssey began on October 24th 1989, with a 3-3 draw at the County Ground. Bolton full-back Phil Brown equalised in injury time. In game two at Burnden Park, Brown scored again in extra time but Duncan Shearer's looping header meant the match finished 1-1. Game three saw the sides meet at Bolton again after a coin toss gave the Trotters choice of venue. Ross MacLaren missed a penalty, but Steve White scored with one of his typical close range finishes. It was 1-1 after extra time, so back to the County Ground it was. By this time it was November 21st 1989. As was traditional, the match went to extra time with the score 1-1, with Ross MacLaren atoning for his missed penalty by netting with just three minutes of extra time left to finally put a dagger through the heart of the contest that refused to die.

FROM ONE END TO THE OTHER

On New Year's Day 1974 Swindon faced Preston North End at home with Town struggling to avoid relegation from Division Two. With the score at 2-1, Frank Burrows punched Mel Holden's shot over the bar to concede a penalty. Burrows was more than happy to take a booking as punishment. Former Swindon striker Ray Treacy stepped up, only to see Jimmy Allan make a full-length diving save. From his clearance, Swindon broke quickly and Dave Moss slid in to finish off Joe Butler's cross and clinch a 3-1 win. The victory was all the sweeter with Treacy, on leaving Swindon for Preston, saying he could hit 20 goals a season in a better side.

TRAINING IS IMPORTANT

In December 1901 Swindon suffered a 10-1 defeat at Kettering Town in the Southern League, but there was an explanation for the scoreline. The main reason was the absence of goalkeeper Bob Menham, who managed to miss his train to Northamptonshire! With no back-up keeper available unfortunate full-back Morton Fagan, known as Paddy, was stuck between the sticks instead. Menham later became a club director despite his indiscretion.

GOING POSTAL

Swindon's match with Sunderland in Division Two in August 1970 was held up for 15 minutes when the goal frame at the Stratton Bank end collapsed after a bruising encounter with Sunderland's Bobby Kerr. Swindon survived the distraction of the posts and bar being put back together and went on to win 2-0 with goals from Arthur Horsfield and Tony Gough.

NOT THEM AGAIN

On-loan goalkeeper Alistair Sperring made his only Swindon appearance in 1984 and it was far from memorable, with Swindon battered 5-1 at home by neighbours Bristol Rovers. After that game Sperring was asked to play in Wednesday's reserve match – against Bristol Rovers! At least he had some joy as Swindon reserves won 3-1, keeping Steve White off the score-sheet. Sperring though, didn't make it into the first team again and left to return to Southampton when his loan was up.

THE WIZARD ON THE WING – DON ROGERS

Don Rogers was a major part of Swindon's success in both the early and late 1960s and has been voted the club's cult hero in a BBC *Football Focus* poll. The winger was signed up by Bert Head as a teenager and made his debut at the age of 17 in the 1962/63 promotion season, before breaking into the side as a regular in the following season and soon looking at ease in Division Two. Rogers was confident with both feet and blessed with a great body swerve that moved him past defenders with apparent ease. He also had a good turn of pace and a finishing ability that appears nonchalant whenever captured on screen. In Danny Williams, Rogers also had a manager who allowed players to express themselves and was happy to see them improvise. Rogers' prolific goalscoring and flair inevitably attracted interest from higher up the pyramid. He did ask for a transfer with his star on the rise and Swindon in Division Three, which puts to bed claims he lacked ambition. In those days though, a board could actually turn down a request and the player was pretty much obliged to stay. Rogers' goalscoring feats were at a peak between 1966 and 1969, when he produced a remarkable 90 goals in three seasons, as well as earning promotion, engineering several giant-killings and earning Wiltshire immortality for his starring role in the 1969 League Cup final win. The club also helped him with the purchase of a sports shop, which he continues to run. Rogers won recognition from the England under-23 squad but sadly never earned a full cap. After a decade of professional football at Swindon, Rogers got his taste of top flight football in 1972, when he was sold to Crystal Palace, managed by Bert Head, for a Swindon record of £147,000, with the club in financial peril. In 1976, Rogers returned to Swindon as part of a deal that saw Peter Eastoe move to Queens Park Rangers. The gate nearly doubled and he marked his return with a goal against Rotherham United. Sadly, Rogers was suffering increasingly with the hip problems that lead to his retirement and ultimately hip replacement surgery, before he retired the season after. A glorious creative force on the pitch, he now has the Don Rogers Stand on the Shrivenham Road side of the ground named after him, a fitting tribute to his role in club history.

THEY PLAY IN RED SO IT MUST BE SWINDON

Swindon fans looking forward to seeing highlights of the 2-0 win at Brentford in December 2003 on HTV's *Soccer Sunday* saw a team running around in red and scoring goals, while the commentary over the top of the picture suggested it was Swindon. The trouble was the match on screen was actually Leyton Orient versus Bury from the same weekend, which also finished 2-0. It seemed neither the difference in ground, kits, nor the lack of similarity between Orient's first goalscorer Gabriel Zakuani and Swindon's Brian Howard alerted those involved to what was going on. HTV went on to issue a public apology for the mistake, blaming a communication error between their offices in Bristol and ITV in London.

HOOLIGANISM

Swindon were no different from any other club in trying to deal with the problem of football hooliganism in the 1970s and 1980s. The problem was addressed in August 1977 by manager Danny Williams who made it clear violence was not welcome. In his programme notes, he wrote: "If you wish to fight join a local boxing club and let us see how brave you are." In March 1978 the visiting Wrexham goalkeeper, Eddie Niedzwecki, was pelted with missiles. Fences were put up. After trouble at a game with Bristol City in 1982 the club announced plans to cover areas of the ground in anti-vandal paint that didn't dry and would stick to the offender's clothes. That didn't solve problems though, with club secretary Bob Jefferies appealing for fans not to be scared off by hooliganism after nasty incidents at a League Cup tie with Bristol Rovers in 1984.

SHANKS SPANKED

Swindon had never met Liverpool until the two sides were paired together in the third round of the 1970/71 League Cup. Bill Shankly was in charge, and while Livepool were still building up to their era of dominance, Swindon faced a side including Ray Clemence, Tommy Smith, Emlyn Hughes and Steve Heighway. A combination of Herculean defending and Don Rogers were too much for Liverpool though – Rogers scored twice in three second-half minutes and Swindon enjoyed another notable League Cup night, winning 2-0.

GOSSIP IS AS OLD AS THE AGES

You might think that talk of who plays and who doesn't, who earns what and who wants to buy who for how much, is a media driven phenomenon with so many different news sources now available. Not so. At the 1920 AGM, one Harold Fleming piped up, the star of the Swindon side. He said that, both in the last season before World War I and the one just gone that the players suffered when there were leaks about who had been selected. At the time, the directors chose the team for the next game on the Monday, but the players weren't informed until the Thursday. Fleming added rumours affected the players' training and he added it wasn't good that players were finding out how others were being paid. He quickly received assurances that such matters would be kept in confidence in the future.

TRES BON-NET

Among the many grounds graced by Swindon, you can add the Parc des Princes. Swindon appeared in a real oddity played in 1910, the Dubonnet Cup. Around 7,000 turned up to watch Swindon and Barnsley play in Paris, in a match designed to increase enthusiasm for amateur football in France. Swindon had reached the FA Cup semi-finals. Barnsley were the losing finalists. Swindon beat Barnsley 2-1 with Harold Fleming scoring both goals to take a very handsome trophy back across the Channel.

THE PENALTY PROBLEM

Swindon were having trouble scoring from the spot at the end of the 1937/38 season, and the problems continued into the pre-season of 1938/39, so manager Ted Vizard decided to try something different when Ben Morton missed in a warm-up match against Newport County. On the Wednesday before the start of the season he put the entire squad through their penalty-taking paces at the County Ground. Sid Swinden was handed the job, but by the time Town finally won a penalty, in their seventh game of the season, he was injured. So, after all that effort to choose a penalty taker it fell to inside-right Cliff Francis to face up to the challenge against Watford – and thankfully he scored.

NON-LEAGUE AND LOOKING LIKE IT

FA Cup exits to non-league teams are just about the most humiliating thing that can happen to a Football League outfit. Being a part of Histon folklore is no fun, so in the interests of proving why a lot of non-league footballers are at that level, it's pleasing to say Swindon have handed out several thrashings to non-league opponents since joining the Football League. The most notable was in 1925, a 10-1 slaughter of Farnham United Breweries, while there were two 7-0 wins in seven years, with Bromley crushed in 1976 and Kettering beaten at their Rockingham Road ground in 1983. Take a bow too Sittingbourne, dismissed 7-0 in the 1920s. Other satisfying wins include a 6-1 victory at Grantham in 1965, while Dulwich Hamlet and Lowestoft have been turned over 6-0. Town had to be content with putting five past Ashford Town (Kent), Gateshead, Newport (Isle of Wight) and Merthyr Tydfil.

A DEBUT A LONG TIME COMING

Swindon striker Craig Maskell had to wait almost five-and-a-half years to finally play for the first team after joining the club. Maskell was signed by Lou Macari on loan from Southampton, while a teenager, for the run in of the 1986/87 season but didn't feature for the first team before heading back to The Dell. Glenn Hoddle brought him in from Reading in the summer of 1992 and Maskell finally pulled on a first team shirt in the opening match of the season at home to Sunderland. Despite being a prolific scorer in the 1992/93 season, Maskell wasn't really to feature in the Premier League, although his late goal at Sheffield Wednesday to earn a point remains a fond memory. Maskell is still involved in the game at non-league level. He's assistant manager at Staines, who he has helped win promotion into the Conference South division for the start of the 2009/10 campaign.

RECORD BREAKER

Swindon's Nicky Summerbee had a successful appearance on the BBC's *Record Breakers* in 1994. The programme was searching for the hardest shot in football and had clearly seen Summerbee strike many a deflected free kick . In a shoot-out with David Burrows, Summerbee's shot registered an impressive 87mph on the speed gun, a pace Burrows couldn't match.

THE PROFITABLE BET THAT PROVED SO COSTLY

In January 1988, Swindon were drawn at Newcastle in the FA Cup, with an overnight stay pretty much a necessity. Swindon would frequently stop at army camps at this point to save money but they couldn't check in to the Catterick garrison so the players ended up staying at the £100 per night Gosforth Park Hotel, costing around £4,000. To cover the costs, almost as a form of insurance, chairman Brian Hillier put a bet on Swindon to lose the game, knowing a win would pay for the expenses in future gate receipts. Swindon lost 5-0 to a top flight Newcastle side with Paul Gascoigne in fine form. The story was splashed over the *Sunday People*. The FA found Hillier guilty of breaking rules on betting. He was fined and banned from football for six months while Macari was fined and warned as to his future conduct, while the club were forced to pay a £7,500 fine. There was never any suggestion the game had been fixed. The incident pre-empted more stories from *The Sunday People*, leading to the illegal payments scandal.

CHAMPIONS: PART TWO – 1995/96

After back-to-back relegations in 1994 and 1995 Swindon were back with a rude thump into the third tier of English football, now known as Division Two. With Premiership parachute payments and the sale of Jan Age Fjortoft, manager Steve McMahon had some money to spend. Signing striker Wayne Allison from rivals Bristol City for £475,000 wasn't universally popular to begin with but 'The Chief' proved to be an excellent investment. Swindon still had Paul Bodin, Shaun Taylor, Kevin Horlock, Martin Ling, Fraser Digby and Ty Gooden from their Premiership squad plus the class of Ian Culverhouse at the back, while a Manchester City reserve team striker Steve Finney proved a big hit up front, especially early in the season as he notched an opening-day winner at Hull City. The quality on show shone through as Town romped home, losing just four league matches all season. A bright start was underlined with two 4-1 wins in a row, over Bradford City and at Bristol Rovers, while Blackburn Rovers needed Alan Shearer to be at his best to avoid a League Cup defeat at the County Ground. Allison settled in well and proved where his loyalties now were by netting in a derby day win over Bristol City. Teams gradually wised up to the fact they couldn't outplay Swindon at home and would come looking for a point. There was a good FA Cup run to go hand-in-hand with the league form. Swindon reached the fifth round before losing to Southampton in a replay, scoring with one of the slickest passing moves you'll see in the home tie. Promotion came at a good place for a party, Blackpool, who had been one of the sides challenging at the top. Kevin Horlock's goal gave Swindon the lead at Bloomfield Road, and Andy Barlow's long-range equaliser couldn't stop Town getting the point they needed to go up. The title was quickly wrapped up at Chesterfield, with four games to go. Peter Thorne and Steve Cowe scored, while Allison tapped in to complete a 3-1 victory. He finished as top-scorer with 20 goals, while Horlock bagged an impressive 16 from his midfield role. There were celebrations, of course, but also a feeling of a job done to right the relegation from the season before. The four league defeats in a season set a new benchmark, while the away form was outstanding, with 13 victories – another club record.

Division Two Final Table

	P	W	D	L	GF	GA	PTS
1. Swindon Town (C)	**46**	**25**	**17**	**4**	**71**	**34**	**92**
2. Oxford United (P)	**46**	**24**	**11**	**11**	**76**	**39**	**83**
3. Blackpool	46	23	13	10	67	40	82
4. Notts County	46	21	15	10	63	39	78
5. Crewe Alexandra	46	22	7	17	77	60	73
6. Bradford City (P)	46	22	7	17	71	69	73

CLEARLY NATURAL SPORTSMEN

As part of their pre-season build-up in 1960, Swindon's footballers took on Swindon Cricket Club in a match to support the town's Carnival and Jubilee celebrations. In a rain affected game, the cricket club players generously declared on 112 for 1, setting the Swindon footballers 113 to win, which they reached with three balls to spare. John Trollope top scored with Ernie Hunt and Keith Morgan there at the end to get the Swindon squad home with three balls to spare.

CRAZY NAME, IMPORTANT GOAL

Colin Todd made several signings in his brief period as Swindon manager. Only the very dedicated will remember Juan Cobian but Australian forward Danny Invincibile caught the imagination and not solely because of his name. Invincibile's most vital contribution came at the end of his first season, when he thumped in a last-minute volley to see off Peterborough United at the end of the 2000/01 season. The 2-1 win gave Swindon a chance of avoiding the drop – Bristol Rovers blew their games in hand and it was the Gas who fell through the trapdoor instead.

Division Two Final Table

	P	W	D	L	GF	GA	PTS
Swindon Town	46	13	13	20	47	65	52
Bristol Rovers (R)	**46**	**12**	**15**	**19**	**53**	**57**	**51**
Luton Town (R)	**46**	**9**	**13**	**24**	**52**	**80**	**40**
Swansea City (R)	**46**	**8**	**13**	**25**	**47**	**73**	**37**
Oxford United (R)	**46**	**7**	**6**	**33**	**53**	**100**	**27**

RAZOR COURTS CONTROVERSY

When Neil 'Razor' Ruddock joined Swindon as player-coach alongside Roy Evans' arrival as manager they were seen as two big-name signings. Ruddock, a bruising defender who revelled in his hard man image, arrived in August 2001 as player-coach. After a struggle to get him sufficiently-sized shorts he scored a cracking free kick on his debut against Colchester United to endear himself to fans. Swindon won the game 1-0. Relations turned sour quickly though as Evans left and Ruddock was kept out of action with a long-term injury. The club ended up turning to the courts to try and get themselves out of his contract. Ruddock ended up acting in kind. At one point he got a High Court injunction out to stop the club being given gate receipts, worth £120,000, from an FA Cup game at Oxford United. Ruddock, who signed a three-year deal, ended up playing just 19 games before he finally reached a deal to have his contract settled early just before an industrial tribunal was due.

SOUTHERN LEAGUE SUCCESS

Before entry into the Football League in 1920, Swindon competed in the Southern League as a fully professional side. They weren't the only ones – the Southern League was highly competitive due to the Football League's northern bias, which was ultimately ended with the top division of the Southern League accepted almost en masse as Division Three in 1920. Swindon twice won the league before World War I, with England international Harold Fleming a key figure on both occasions. In defence, Swindon had Scottish international Jock Walker and the highly-regarded Billy Silto. The first title came in the 1910/11 season, when 7,000 spectators turned up to see the decisive game against nearest rivals Brighton & Hove Albion. Billy Tout scored with a twice-taken penalty, Freddy Wheatcroft headed in a corner, with Harold Fleming adding a third to clinch the title at home. In 1914 though, Fleming was missing for the final game of the season at Cardiff City. Again, Swindon had faltered, after winning their opening ten games. A 0-0 draw at Ninian Park proved to be just enough for Swindon to win the Southern Shield for the second time, thanks to an excellent display from goalkeeper Len Skiller. Swindon finished just ahead of Crystal Palace on the sometimes mysterious goal average calculation. The returning team were greeted enthusiastically at Swindon railway station on their arrival.

Southern League 1910/11

	P	W	D	L	GF	GA	PTS
Swindon Town (C)	**38**	**24**	**5**	**9**	**80**	**31**	**53**
Northampton Town	38	18	12	8	54	27	48
Brighton & Hove Albion	38	20	8	10	58	36	48
Crystal Palace	38	17	13	8	55	48	47

Southern League 1913/14

	P	W	D	L	GF	GA	PTS
Swindon Town (C)	**38**	**21**	**8**	**9**	**81**	**41**	**50**
Crystal Palace	38	17	16	5	60	32	50
Northampton Town	38	14	19	5	50	37	47
Reading	38	17	10	11	43	36	44

HE'LL COST MORE THAN YOU BARGAINED FOR

Swindon found themselves taking on much more than they anticipated when they signed French winger Sebastien Ruster in October 2003 after he had impressed while on trial. Ruster came to the County Ground after a recommendation from Peter Reid and the Frenchman was thought to be a free agent after being released by Cannes. Once Ruster was signed up on a permanent contract Cannes demanded compensation, saying they had only let Ruster go after the loss of their professional status. FIFA agreed and said Swindon should stump up a sum, way beyond expectations, of €345,000, a sum the current board simply couldn't afford. Ruster returned to France in January having started one game, against Boston United in the LDV Vans Trophy tie. Swindon then won a significant victory by going above FIFA, to the Court of Arbitration for Sport in Lausanne, to appeal against the judgement. The sum due was reduced massively, to just €20,000.

TON UP

Swindon have scored 100 league goals in a season just once since election into the Football League. That was in Division Three (South) in the 1926/27 season. Harry Morris made it 100 in the last game of the campaign, a win at home to Queens Park Rangers. A leaky defence, which shipped 85 goals, meant promotion was beyond them. The reverse, conceding 100 goals, has been done twice. In 1932/33, Swindon finished bottom of Division Three, having 105 goals put past three different keepers. In the Premier League, it was exactly 100 against, after injuries forced John Gorman to use four different shot stoppers in Fraser Digby, Nicky Hammond, Jon Sheffield and Paul Heald. The hundredth came in the last game, as the hapless Heald was unable to stem a flow of goals from Leeds United.

CAN'T STOP SCORING

Winger Bobby Barnes had an impressive purple patch shortly after his arrival from Aldershot in 1987. He scored in six straight league matches against Manchester City, Leicester City, Plymouth Argyle, Leeds United, AFC Bournemouth and Huddersfield Town. Despite his impressive individual run of form it was only in the last two of those games that Swindon secured maximum points.

IT'S GOOD TO BE BACK – OR IS IT?

Several Swindon players from successful sides have come back for a second
– and even third – spell at the County Ground, with varying results.

Paul Bodin	1988/91	119 apps, 10 goals
	1992/96	188 apps, 30 goals
Andy Gurney	2001/04	145 apps, 23 goals
	2005/06	31 apps, 2 goals
Chris Kamara	1977/81	184 apps, 26 goals
	1985/88	114 apps, 6 goals
David Kerslake*	1989/93	165 apps, 1 goal
	1997/99	22 apps, 0 goals
Phil King	1987/89	145 apps, 4 goals
	1997	5 apps, 0 goals
Martin Ling	1986	2 apps, 0 goals
	1991/96	189 apps, 13 goals
Alan Mayes	1979/80	112 apps, 51 goals
	1983/85	72 apps, 32 goals
David Moss	1972/78	270 apps, 81 goals
	1985/86	5 apps, 1 goal
Jimmy Quinn*	1981/84	60 apps, 18 goals
	1986/88	76 apps, 43 goals
Paul Rideout	1980/83	105 apps, 41 goals
	1991	9 apps, 1 goal
Don Rogers	1962/72	474 apps, 179 goals
	1976/77	16 games, 2 goals
Nicky Summerbee	1989/94	135 apps, 10 goals
	2005	1 app, 0 goals
Adrian Viveash	1990/95	64 apps, 3 goals
	2003/04	17 apps, 0 goals

*David Kerslake and Jimmy Quinn had three playing stints. Kerslake returned
on loan in November 1996 from Spurs, playing eight times before signing on
a free transfer that summer. Quinn came out of retirement for eight games
during his spell as boss. Paul Bodin's departure proved good business. He was
sold to Crystal Palace for £550,000 in March 1991. The next January he was
back at the County Ground, for less than half the price – £225,000.

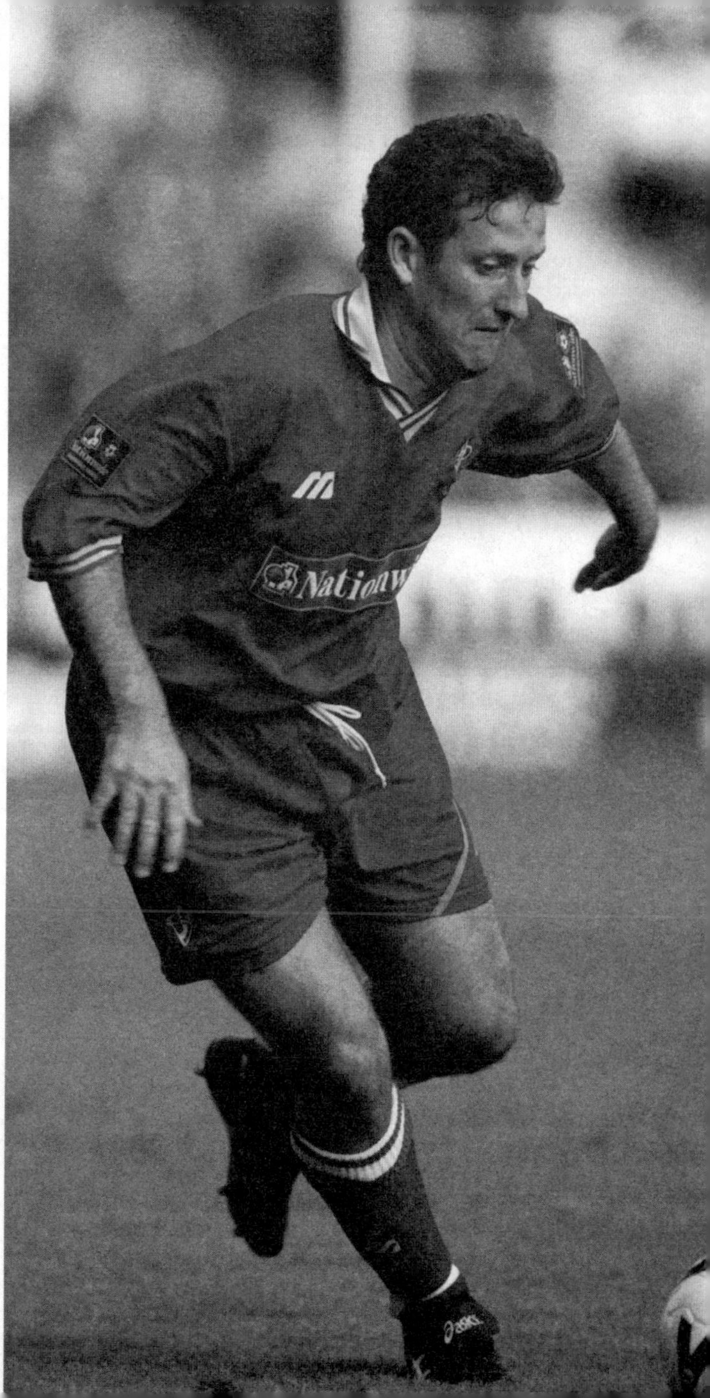

DAVID KERSLAKE: SECOND TIME ROUND

THE LATE, LATE, LATE, LATE SHOW

Swindon's only ever trip to Kidderminster Harriers, in the LDV Vans Trophy on November 12th 2002, produced what is surely the latest finish to a game in England. A nearby power failure meant that, at first, the Aggborough floodlights couldn't flicker into life. The game was eventually given the go ahead by referee Trevor Parkes at around 9pm. With the match level at 2-2 after 90 minutes the Swindon scorers were Danny Invincibile and Alan Young. So, on it was to extra time and even later into the evening. Finally, Abdou Sall scored for Kidderminster with a header after 105 minutes of play. With the golden goal rule applying, it meant everyone could finally pack up and go home just after 11pm.

MUCH STILL TO BE CONQUERED

Going into the 2009/10 season, Swindon had still to record a win in a competitive match at 17 of the 92 current Football League clubs. Town have never emerged from the homes of Liverpool, Chelsea, Arsenal, Tottenham Hotspur, Everton, Newcastle United, Derby County, Nottingham Forest, Doncaster Rovers, Leeds United, Cheltenham Town, Barnet, Accrington Stanley, Macclesfield Town or Dagenham & Redbridge celebrating victory. Swindon have never played at Morecambe or Burton Albion.

THE ONE THAT GOT AWAY

In March 1964, Swindon were all set to sign a prolific goal scorer for Wiltshire Schools by the name of Mick Channon. Manager Bert Head had arranged to go and see him on a Monday to complete the deal. However, Southampton got a tip-off from the manager of Channon's club at youth level. The Saints manager Ted Bates went to Channon's house on the Sunday beforehand. Although the rules said that players could not be signed as professionals on a Sunday, the Saints found a way round that by putting Channon on amateur forms to begin with. He went on to be Southampton's all-time record scorer as well as netting 21 times in 46 games for England. It would not be the last time that Swindon and Southampton would be in competition for young talent – Theo Walcott is one of many names that springs to mind.

A SENSATIONAL START

Swindon were heading into the unknown as they began a first-ever Second Division campaign in the 1963/64 season – but there was no shortage of confidence. The start they made was jaw dropping. Bert Head's side began the season with six wins in a row, including a memorable 3-0 home victory over Manchester City, who had just been relegated. The first points dropped were at Leeds United in a 0-0 draw, but that was against a side including Billy Bremner, Jackie Charlton, Johnny Giles and Norman Hunter. Swindon were still unbeaten after nine games and top of the table, but they then suffered a heavy 4-0 loss at home to Northampton Town, the side who had come up with them. In the end Town failed to follow up their promise and finished in mid-table, in fourteenth place.

HISTORY REPEATS ITSELF, YET DOESN'T

The 1939/40 season was abandoned after just three games due to the start of World War II. Swindon started with defeats to Northampton Town and Cardiff City and a home draw with Aldershot. When league football resumed in 1946/47, the league stuck to the 1939/40 fixtures. Though Swindon lost at Northampton again, they beat Cardiff 3-2 and crushed Aldershot 7-0 – a much better start. Only one Swindon player, outside-right Eddie Jones, played in both of those defeats by the Cobblers.

ATTENDANCE RECORD

The highest official attendance at the County Ground is 31,668, for the FA Cup tie with Arsenal on January 15th 1972. Most left disappointed as Swindon lost 2-0. The largest league crowd was 28,898 on March 29th 1969 as Swindon met Watford with both sides going for the Division Three title. The away side came through 1-0 winners.

STUMPING UP TO SPONSOR

In 1983 ISIS became the first company to have their name on Swindon shirts. Other companies to follow were Lowndes Lambert, radio station GWR, oil giants Burmah and Castrol, the Swindon-based Nationwide Building Society, Kingswood Group and most recently, *Four Four Two* magazine.

THE ACRIMONIOUS END OF ENDERSBY

Swindon goalkeeper Scott Endersby effectively turned down the chance to play for Swindon against Division One side Sheffield Wednesday in the Milk Cup third round in 1985. Endersby was growing increasingly frustrated at being relegated to second choice behind new signing Kenny Allen. He was the previous year's Player of the Season. Allen couldn't play in the competition after turning out for Torquay United – against Swindon – in round one. Endersby had featured in round two, where Town knocked out Sunderland, only to lose his place for the following league game. This brought Endersby's frustrations to a head. Manager Lou Macari claimed that Endersby said he wouldn't play in the Milk Cup match unless the club granted him a free transfer, even though he was transfer listed and Swindon wanted a 'small fee' for him. Endersby says the fee wasn't small and exercised a clause in his contract to hand in his notice. Both sides stood their ground. Endersby didn't play and Macari, after a brief attempt to contact Pat Jennings, brought in the Brentford keeper Richard Key on a non-contract basis. Key kept a clean sheet and Swindon came away with another League Cup shock, a 1-0 win.

PLAYER OF THE YEAR? I'M OUT OF HERE

Winning the Swindon Town Player of the Year award in recent seasons has been prompted by the trophy-holder making a rapid exit from the County Ground. The trend started with Tommy Mooney in 2003/04, who claimed a contract offer from the club had not been honoured. He ended up signing for Oxford United, where he was unable to fully recapture his prolific Swindon form. The following season saw striker Sam Parkin win the award, but he was off, understandably, to test himself at a higher level, signing for Ipswich Town. In 2005/06, goalkeeper Rhys Evans, a Swindon native, was one of the more effective performers in a season of relegation. The lure of a contract by the seaside at Blackpool, still in League One, was too much. Lee Peacock bucked the trend by staying at the end of 2006/07, but full back Miguel Comminges, signed by Paul Sturrock, was off after winning the 2007/08 award. Having impressed with some attacking performances, the man from Guadeloupe joined Cardiff City.

A CUP OF LITTLE CHEER

Swindon have had great days in the League Cup and FA Cup, but there has been little joy in the Associate Members Cup in its many guises as the Auto Windscreens Shield, the Johnstone's Paint Trophy and so on. Swindon's first match in the competition is perhaps as good as it gets – a win at Oxford United. The competition saw Swindon's first penalty shoot-out – a defeat at Torquay United. A good run in 1987 was ended by a controversial home loss against Aldershot after Fraser Digby was sent off, while in 2001 Swindon were the last Division Two team in the Southern section, but lost at Southend United. That was made up for by a 6-1 slaughter of Southend in 2002 that left Shrimpers manager Rob Newman almost incoherent through rage. It's been back to normal service since, with exits at the likes of Boston United and Kidderminster Harriers, while defeat at Brighton & Hove Albion in 2008 brought the end of Maurice Malpas' time in charge of the club. Town have yet to even reach the regional final, let alone go to Wembley or Cardiff. Thirty-two different players have scored in Swindon colours in the competition, including the late Jimmy Davis and such relative County Ground obscurities as Ibon Arrieta, Chris Blackburn and Alan Young.

SPECIAL DAYS IN FRONT OF GOAL

Here's a list of Swindon players who have scored four goals or more in a game since World War II. Keith East's nine goals on consecutive Saturdays will take some beating:

Bill Stephens 4	Swindon 7 Aldershot 0	Sep 7th 1946
Maurice Owen 4	Swindon 6 Mansfield 1	Mar 1st 1947
David Layne 4	Bath City 4 Swindon 6	Nov 9th 1960
Keith East 4	Swindon 5 Merthyr Tydfil 1	Nov 13th 1965
Keith East 5	Swindon 6 Mansfield 2	Nov 20th 1965
Dennis Brown 4	Bournemouth 4 Swindon 1	Oct 29th 1966
Don Rogers 4	Swindon 5 Southport 1	Nov 2nd 1968
Andy Rowland 4	Swindon 6 Rotherham 2	Apr 15th 1980
Duncan Shearer 4	Plymouth 4 Swindon 0	Oct 5th 1991

WORLD WAR II

Swindon played wartime football in 1939/40, but the club was effectively closed down in 1940 when the government requisitioned the County Ground. A brief public statement said that the ground was simply needed for "other purposes". The club was to cease playing, according to secretary Sam Allen "until further notice". Fixtures and fittings at the County Ground were sold off. During the wartime years huts were put on the pitch, on the Shrivenham Road side, for housing prisoners of war, a state of affairs that lasted for almost five years, with the condition of the ground during that time taking second place to the greater effort. The West Stand was converted into an air-raid shelter. It meant the club effectively had to be restarted almost from scratch for the 1946/7 season, a problem that didn't affect some other clubs. A search for a new manager was also put in place with pre-war boss Neil Harris dying in 1940.

REFEREE ACCOUNTABILITY – FOR ONE NIGHT ONLY

Swindon started the 1989/90 season with a home defeat to Sunderland that saw four players booked, including player-manager Ossie Ardiles, while Fitzroy Simpson was sent off after two yellows in three minutes by referee Tony Ward. A group of not-too-impressed Swindon supporters in exile went to a London Football Supporters Club meeting the Monday afterwards. They were intrigued to find out the guest speaker, on refereeing, was none other than Tony Ward. This chance to grill an official first-hand revealed, among other things, the colourful language Simpson had used to earn his second yellow.

NOT THE AVERAGE MASCOT

Swindon's mascot for the game with Exeter City on October 1st 1985 was not quite your usual fresh-faced youngster. She was no less than the national holder of the Miss Lovely Legs title, Anna Dinning. The 19-year-old, who also held the post of Miss Thamesdown, was keen to lead out Swindon ahead of a match before stepping down from her arduous duties. She clearly had a positive effect. Colin Calderwood scored the winner with a minute to go to earn Swindon a 2-1 victory, Town's first in five matches.

MAURICE OWEN

Maurice Owen was a truly loyal Swindon servant of the 1950s and 1960s. Striker Owen was spotted playing at Abingdon Town, having served as a soldier in Burma in the Second World War. He showed an eye for goal immediately, beginning life with a hat-trick against Watford and hitting four goals in a 6-1 win over Mansfield Town in his debut season in 1946/47. Owen went on to make more than 500 appearances for Swindon, a club record which lasted until John Trollope came on to the scene. Happy near Abingdon, he turned down moves to other clubs higher up the football pyramid – notably Norwich – while an effort to sell him to Bristol City also fell through. Despite playing in a pretty modest team in Division Three (South), Owen's talents were sufficiently recognised for him to be capped at England 'B' level. In the latter stages of his career, Owen dropped back into central defence, which suited him as an outstanding header of the ball. His playing career ended in perfect style with Swindon winning promotion for the first time in 1962/63. The respect for his ability was shown in some of the names of the All-Star team who played in his testimonial game. They included Billy Wright, Tom Finney and Roger Hunt. After his playing career finished, Owen took up several roles behind the scenes at the County Ground. He was a coach and he also had a spell as groundsman before his retirement in 1984. He even took his pay-off, of £100, in good humour.

STARS OF THE FUTURE

Two big-name Premiership players made their league debuts while on loan at Swindon. With Fraser Digby injured at the start of the 1995/96 season, Steve McMahon brought in the Blackburn goalkeeper Shay Given on loan. The young Irishman helped Swindon to four wins in five games, keeping four clean sheets. He's since gone on to play in the Champions League for Newcastle and be the first choice for the Republic of Ireland in the 2002 World Cup. In 1999, Jimmy Quinn signed the West Ham United teenager Michael Carrick, who made his first competitive start in a Swindon shirt. Carrick played six games, scoring twice. At the time of writing Carrick is a first-team regular for Manchester United, who paid £18.6m for his services.

SUMMERTIME BUT THE LIVING IS NOT SO EASY

As late as the 1960s, players would have summer jobs to boost their earnings from football in the off-season. Ernie Hunt, despite being very much a star in the making, had some odder choices than most. Hunt would spend many afternoons cutting hair at a local salon, something his father had done in the local factories. Hunt also spent one summer as a gravedigger just before he turned professional, alongside his good friend Mike Summerbee.

SOME CROWD FOR THE STIFFS

Swindon reserves attracted a gate of 12,788 for their game with Birmingham City on January 18th 1977. Naturally though, there was an ulterior motive. Vouchers were being issued at the game for the forthcoming FA Cup match with Everton. The voucher system wasn't a huge success either, leading to several complaints. For the record Swindon reserves beat Birmingham's second string, including Kenny Burns, 2-0.

MY CUP ALMOST RUNNETH OVER

Swindon's best FA Cup runs both came in the Southern League era, with a Harold Fleming-inspired side reaching the last four in 1910 and 1912. In the 1909/10 season Swindon saw off Crystal Palace, Burnley, Spurs and Manchester City to earn a semi-final with Newcastle United at White Hart Lane. Freddy Wheatcroft came closest for Swindon when he hit the post, but Newcastle scored twice in three minutes in the second half. In the 1911/12 season Sutton Junction, Notts County, West Ham United (after a replay) and Everton were conquered, with Swindon notching an impressive 2-1 quarter-final win over the team from Merseyside. It saw Swindon paired with Barnsley in the semi-finals, a repeat of their Dubonnet Cup meeting. The first game finished 0-0. Swindon were without Harold Fleming for the replay after he'd been battered by the Tykes in the first match – he was put out of action for nearly a year. With the national papers moved to comment on the physical edge to Barnsley's play, they won the replay 1-0 at Meadow Lane after Archie Bown missed a penalty.

Swindon's best run as a Football League side came in the 1969/70 season, making the last eight before a home defeat by Leeds United.

1909/10 FA Cup Run

Round/Scorers	Opponents	Score
First round ....Crystal Palace (A)		3-1
Tout, Fleming, Bown		
Second round ....Burnley (H)		2-0
Bown, Fleming		
Third round ....Tottenham Hotspur (H)		3-2
Fleming (3)		
Quarter-final ....Manchester City (H)		2-0
Jefferson, Bown		
Semi-final...........................Newcastle United (White Hart Lane)....		0-2
None		

1911/12 FA Cup Run

Round/Scorers	Opponents	Score
First round ....Sutton Junction (H).................................		5-0
Fleming (4), Bown		
Second round ....Notts County (H)......................................		2-0
Jefferson, Wheatcroft		
Third round ....West Ham United (A)		1-1
Fleming		
Third round replay ....West Ham United (H).............................		4-0
Glover (og x 2), Jefferson, Wheatcroft		
Quarter-final ....Everton (H)..		2-1
Jefferson, Bown		
Semi-final...........................Barnsley (Stamford Bridge)		0-0
None		
Semi-final replay ....Barnsley (Meadow Lane)..........................		0-1
None		

NIGHTMARE ON FILBERT STREET

Swindon had three all too eventful encounters with Leicester City in four years that got dubbed as the "Nightmares on Filbert Street". The sequence started on November 7th 1987. Swindon had gone 1-0 up and had extended the lead to 2-0 after Jimmy Quinn followed up his penalty that had initially been saved by spot-kick specialist Paul Cooper and Swindon were looking good for victory despite a red card for Steve Foley. Then there were three goals in the last eight minutes, with Swindon collapsing to a 3-2 defeat with Mark Venus scoring an injury-time winner. Less than a year later, on October 26th 1988, things went pear-shaped again. Swindon sprinted into a 3-0 lead with a goal from Phil King, a superb long range volley from Steve White and a third from Charlie Henry. It was time for history to repeat itself as Foley was sent off. Then came the comeback. Gary McAllister scored a soft penalty, there was a bizarre own goal from Phil King and McAllister made it 3-3 with a quarter of an hour left. Things managed to get even worse, with Tom Jones sent off for a second bookable offence, but at least Swindon managed to hang on for a point this time. After a relatively normal 2-1 reverse in 1989, things were back to normal for the midweek trip to Leicester on October 24th 1990. David Kerslake was dismissed after three minutes for a tackle on Tommy Wright on the halfway line. Duncan Shearer's header and Steve White's opportunism put Swindon 2-0 up, but Ally Mauchlen's shot and an injury-time thunderbolt from Marc North meant yet another Leicester comeback was complete. Perhaps something from Filbert Street hung over the Walkers Stadium after it was demolished. Swindon's first visit there saw yet another late Leicester equaliser.

THE DEFINITIVE HAT-TRICK

Kevin Horlock produced about as close as you can get to the perfect hat-trick from a Swindon player in 1995. Firstly, it was away in a local derby at Bristol Rovers, or, to be accurate, at Twerton Park, Bath. Secondly, it helped Swindon to a crushing 4-1 win. Thirdly, it consisted of scoring with three different parts of the Horlock anatomy. There was one finish with his right foot, another with his left, and a header.

A RIOT AND A ROUT

In 1970, Swindon reached the final of the Anglo Italian Cup, coming through the qualifying phase to take on Napoli in the final. The group stage had produced the immortal result of Swindon 4 Juventus 0. The match took place in Naples on May 28th 1970 and Swindon were soon in control against their Serie A opponents. Peter Noble headed Swindon in front before half-time. He added another in the second half and Arthur Horsfield then struck a third. Either all this was too much for the home fans, or something predetermined happened, as irate Napoli supporters started to tear up the concrete benches and hurl the pieces on to the pitch. In increasing chaos, the referee Paul Schiller abandoned the match with just over ten minutes to go. Despite the anarchy, Swindon were still presented with the trophy and manager Fred Ford, in an act of bravery or foolhardiness, went to the Italian fans to show them the cup. Whilst many applauded, the trouble continued. The players managed to escape to safety and make it to the dressing rooms, while the rioting eventually spread to outside the stadium. Afterwards, referee Schiller, who had taken charge in several Fairs Cup matches, complimented Swindon on the quality of their performance.

GOING UP: PART FIVE 2006/07

Swindon's last promotion, to date, came despite increasing anarchy off-field and a change of manager. After slipping down into the bottom division for just the second time in the club's history, Dennis Wise arrived as manager in the summer of 2006 and his side started with six straight league wins, including a last minute victory over Barnet, but his reign lasted 17 matches and saw director Bob Holt resign after speaking about a meeting with Wise in public. Wise left to join Leeds United in October, firing a parting shot at the board in his last interviews. Coach Adrian Williams briefly took charge before the appointment of Paul Sturrock in November, who had a good track record in earning promotion with Plymouth Argyle and Sheffield Wednesday. His team gradually ground out wins, becoming the first side to beat Walsall at home in a 2-0 victory at the Bescot Stadium in December while there was a key 1-0 defeat of the MK Dons on New Year's Day, which saw keeper Phil Smith, signed from non-league Crawley Town, save a penalty. A run of two victories in seven in February and March saw the side drop out of the top three for a period, with manager Sturrock particularly unimpressed by a 1-0 defeat at Barnet. It saw the Scotsman sign five players in the final week before the transfer deadline shut, most notably striker Barry Corr. The key game came at Lincoln City, just above Swindon in the table at the time. Corr made his debut and after falling behind Swindon scored three times. The game finished 3-2. Teenage striker Lukas Jutkiewicz weighed in with important late goals against Torquay United and Bury to keep the momentum going. Swindon had a chance to clinch promotion in their penultimate match at Bristol Rovers, but lost 1-0, meaning there was a chance they could still be caught by Milton Keynes. It meant everything rested on the final game at home to Walsall, where a point was needed to guarantee promotion, while the Saddlers wanted to clinch the League Two title. The County Ground erupted in joy and relief and when defender Jerel Ifil headed in a second-half corner Swindon were almost there. An injury time free kick gave Walsall the championship and all four corners of the ground had something to savour after a 1-1 draw. It meant Paul Sturrock had completed the task he was appointed to do; making sure Swindon's second stay in the bottom division was as brief as possible.

League Two Final Table

	P	W	D	L	GF	GA	PTS
Walsall (C)	46	25	14	7	66	34	89
Hartlepool United (P)	46	26	10	10	65	40	88
Swindon Town (P)	46	25	10	11	58	38	85
MK Dons	46	25	9	12	76	58	84
Lincoln City	46	21	11	14	70	59	74

FAR FROM CHRISTMAS TURKEYS

No matter how well, or badly, the season is going, Swindon fans can look forward to Christmas after winning their last five matches on Boxing Day going into the 2009/10 season. The 2008 Boxing Day match at Leyton Orient was particularly festive, with Lee Peacock scoring with a terrific drive inside 60 seconds on the day the appointment of Danny Wilson as manager was confirmed. Swindon won 2-1 in a game rich on entertainment. The sequence began in 2004 with Sam Parkin and Sammy Igoe scoring Swindon's goals in a 2-0 win over Peterborough United at London Road. Next up were Colchester United, then Wycombe Wanderers, and in 2007 there was a West Country win down the road at Yeovil Town thanks to a goal from Barry Corr.

SO MANY SPANKINGS

Despite the appointment of Bert Head midway through the season, 1956/57 was a dismal campaign for Swindon Town in Division Three (South) with the defence at times producing some horror shows; they had seven goals put past them three times in league fixtures. On September 22nd 1956 there was a 7-0 defeat at Bournemouth & Boscombe, with Sam Burton in goal. Just after Christmas came a 7-3 loss at Gay Meadow against Shrewsbury Town. At this point, Ray Chandler was the unfortunate keeper. The third and final battering that season was in a 7-0 loss at Torquay United, with Burton back but powerless to prevent the rout.

LEADING FA CUP SCORERS

Harold Fleming	19
Jimmy Pugh	16
Dick Jones	15
Maurice Owen	15
Harry Morris	14
Dave Moss	14
Don Rogers	12
Robbie Reynolds	11
Andy Rowland	11
Archie Bown	10
Frank Richardson	10

FEELING THE PRESSURE?

Swindon's first ever £1,000 player was striker Ben Morton, signed from Torquay United in October 1937 by Ted Vizard. Clearly the transfer fee caused a level of expectation, but Morton couldn't find the net, in a Fjortoft-like barren spell, for his first 11 matches. Finally, in game number 12, Morton was close to drawing another blank, but with five minutes to go, and Swindon about to go out of the FA Cup, came that elusive first goal. It came against Grimsby Town, who were in Division One at the time, and Swindon went on to knock their opponents out of the cup in extra time. Morton really only came to the fore next season, hitting 32 goals in 44 games, before the arrival of the Second World War robbed him of the best years of his career.

MULTI SPORT MAN

Swindon manager Louis Page was keen on signing Arsenal wing-half Ralph Prouton in August 1952, so naturally he went off to meet his man. Luckily he wasn't too busy, as he was acting as twelfth man for Hampshire against Sussex in a County Championship game at Portsmouth. It meant he was able to sign the necessary forms during the match. Prouton's summer job was as Hampshire's wicketkeeper and his cricket career lasted longer than his Swindon one.

OLDHAM NIL, EVERYBODY ELSE SOMETHING

Swindon really struggled defensively in the 2008/9 season, especially under Maurice Malpas. It took 17 games before the first clean sheet of the season finally arrived, in a 2-0 win home over Oldham Athletic. It took another 16 games before Swindon would manage the feat again, by which time Malpas had been dismissed and Danny Wilson had taken charge. The opponents, strangely enough, were Oldham, who Swindon shut out in a 0-0 game at Boundary Park. Swindon faced 26 different teams in the campaign – the other 25 all managed to score past Phil Smith or Peter Brezovan.

BADGE OF HONOUR

The club's badge has changed several times throughout history. There has been a simple badge with a robin in the centre and the letters STFC in each corner, while the main variations are a shield which would usually include a robin and a train, reflecting the club's nickname and Swindon's railway history. A departure from this was the 'traffic sign' design of the 1970s featuring the letters 'S' and 'T' becoming interlocked in a sequence of arrows. After a return to a more traditional crest badge a new logo was introduced following the early 1990s financial problems and demotion by the Football League. It featured the letter 'S' in a green and red diamond with arrows going through the middle behind a football. It was designed to imply forward thinking and progress. This rather anodyne creation lasted until 2007, where fans were asked to vote on three designs which saw a crest re-introduced. Again a robin and a train featured in all three, with the re-introduction of the motto *Salubritas et Industria* – health and industry, the motto of the town of Swindon, as well as the football club.

SIMOD SAYS

Swindon had some good moments in the Full Members Cup, known as the Simod Cup and the Zenith Data Systems Cup which flickered into life in the 1980s when English clubs were banned from Europe. In the 1987/88 season Swindon had three wins over First Division opposition, most notably a 4-0 thumping of Chelsea at the County Ground. Norwich City were beaten 2-1 in the quarter-finals but a defeat at Luton denied Town a trip to Wembley. The Canaries were to become familiar opponents in the competition's brief life, with Swindon drawn to face them in three consecutive seasons, winning two of those matches.

X MARKS THE SPOT

When Swindon won the 1995/96 Division Two title, they set an unexpected club record: the most draws ever in a league season, with 17 matches ending all square. Ten came at home. Swindon's last-minute draw at Peterborough United at the end of the 2008/09 season equalled that total. This time Swindon finished in a more modest fifteenth position.

SICK OF THE SIGHT OF SHREW

Swindon played Shrewsbury Town no less than seven times in 1960. The two sides first met in the league in March, with Swindon winning 4-2 thanks to a Bronco Layne hat-trick which was to be the only victory in the sequence. There was a league draw as the season started up again in August, followed by draws in both legs of a League Cup tie. Bronco Layne's leveller at Gay Meadow in the second leg meant a replay, which Shrewsbury won at the County Ground after extra time. The sides were also paired together in the FA Cup, with the Shrews winning 1-0 in Wiltshire. Finally, they met in the league again on New Year's Eve; Bobby Woodruff scored twice in a 2-2 draw.

ABACUS PLEASE

The highest-scoring league match in Swindon history took place at Brighton & Hove Albion's Goldstone Ground on September 18th 1926, when Swindon were beaten 9-3. Joe Eddleston (2) and Charlie Petrie scored the Swindon goals.

I'VE STARTED, BUT AS FOR THE FINISH...

Back-to-back seasons under Steve McMahon in Division One saw two truly terrible finishes to the campaign. In 1996/97, McMahon's side won just one of their final 11 matches. Then in 1997/98, the run-in blues arrived even earlier, to the point where they weren't run-in blues at all. It was one win in the last 13 league games.

	P	W	D	L	GF	GA	PTS
1996/97	11	1	3	7	3	25	6
1997/98	13	1	3	9	7	27	6

Among the spectacular defeats in the two sequences were a 7-0 loss at Bolton Wanderers, a 6-0 loss at Middlesbrough, plus other 5-1, 5-0 and 4-0 reverses.

JIMMY DAVIS RIP

Jimmy Davis joined Swindon on loan from Manchester United at the start of the 2002/03 season. The winger enjoyed his spell at the County Ground, playing 15 games, scoring three times. His eagerness to run with the ball saw him become popular with fans – he got a standing ovation when he came off in his final game, at home to Tranmere Rovers, and gave one supporter his boots. Attempts to get him back for future loan spells, though, proved unsuccessful, with Sir Alex Ferguson keen to see Davis test himself at a higher level than Swindon could offer. The 2003/04 campaign began in the worst possible way. Davis, now on loan with Watford, died following a car crash on the M40 in the small hours of the Saturday morning when the season was due to begin. While Watford's game was postponed, Swindon played Sheffield Wednesday at home on the opening day in what were awful circumstances for everyone involved. Just a fortnight later, Jimmy's mother, Jenny Burton, came to the County Ground ahead of the game with Notts County and gave an on-pitch speech thanking the fans for just how welcome he was made during his stay in Wiltshire. There was also one minute's silence in his memory. Swindon also supported the Jimmy Davis Memorial Cup in 2004, when they travelled to Redditch United, Davis' home-town club, for a pre-season friendly, with the money raised going to support local youth football.

TURNING OVER THE TOP FLIGHT

Here's a list of Swindon wins over top-division opponents in cup competitions. Note the rather long time since the last entry.

1907/08	3-2 v Sheffield United (H)	FA Cup second round
1910/11	3-1 v Notts County (H)	FA Cup first round
1910/11	1-0 v Woolwich Arsenal (H)	FA Cup second round
1911/12	2-0 v Notts County (H)	FA Cup second round
1911/12	2-1 v Everton (H)	FA Cup quarter-final
1920/21	1-0 v Sheffield United (H)	FA Cup first round
1928/29	2-0 v Newcastle United (H)	FA Cup third round
1928/29	3-2 v Burnley (H)	FA Cup fourth round
1929/30	2-0 v Manchester United (A)	FA Cup third round
1937/38	2-1 v Grimsby Town (H)*	FA Cup third round
1947/48	2-0 v Burnley (A)	FA Cup third round
1951/52	1-0 v Stoke City (A)	FA Cup fourth round
1961/62	2-0 v Birmingham City (H)	League Cup first round
1963/64	3-0 v Chelsea (H)	League Cup second round
1966/67	3-1 v West Ham United (H)	FA Cup third round
1968/69	3-0 v Coventry City (H)	League Cup third round
1968/69	2-1 v Burnley (H)	League Cup semi-final first leg
1968/69	3-2 v Burnley (The Hawthorns)*	League Cup semi-final R
1968/69	3-1 v Arsenal (Wembley)*	League Cup Final
1970/71	2-0 v Liverpool (H)	League Cup third round
1972/73	2-0 v Birmingham City (H)	FA Cup third round
1979/80	2-1 v Stoke City (H)	League Cup third round
1979/80	4-3 v Arsenal (H)*	League Cup quarter-final
1979/80	2-1 v Wolves (H)	League Cup semi-final
1985/86	1-0 v Sheffield Wednesday (H)	League Cup third round
1987/88	2-0 v Norwich City (A)	FA Cup third round
1987/88	2-1 v Derby County (H)	Simod Cup second round
1987/88	4-0 v Chelsea (H)	Simod Cup third round
1987/88	2-0 v Norwich City (H)	Simod Cup quarter-final
1989/90	2-1 v Millwall (H)	ZDS Cup second round
1989/90	4-1 v Norwich City (H)	ZDS Cup quarter-final

*indicates extra time win

MANCUNIAN MASTERY AND MAYHEM

In the 1929/30 season Swindon had joy and despair in Manchester. In the FA Cup third round, Swindon upset Manchester United 2-0 at Old Trafford, to record the club's first ever win at a top division side. Joe Eddleston scored inside the first half-hour, and Les Roberts added a second, with Swindon holding firm to claim that historic win. The fourth round saw Swindon paired with United's neighbours Manchester City, who would end the season in third place in Division One. After a 1-1 draw at home, with City's Phil McCloy kindly putting through his own net, it was off to Maine Road for the replay. Swindon lost 10-1 in what remains the club's joint-record defeat and worst-ever reverse in a cup competition. Harry Morris scored Swindon's lone goal.

KING OF THE QUOTES

Post-match interviews with cigar-loving Swindon boss Andy King would often contain something out of the ordinary, but this is one of his more bizarre analyses of a frustrating performance: "I thought we started very, very brightly but the Achilles heel which has bitten us in the backside all year has stood out like a sore thumb."

LEADING LEAGUE CUP SCORERS

The Jack Smith listed is the forward who played for the club between 1961 and 64, rather than the full-back released in the summer of 2009.

1 Don Rogers	17
2= Duncan Shearer	11
2= Steve White	11
4= Alan Mayes	10
4= Roger Smart	10
6 Jan Age Fjortoft	9
7= Dave Moss	8
7= Jimmy Quinn	8
7= Andy Rowland	8
7= Jack Smith	8

OVERSEAS XI

This 11 is made up of Swindon's overseas contingent:

Peter Brezovan........................goalkeeper.................Slovakia..........2006/09
Frederic Darras.......................right-back.................France............1996/97
Antoine Van Der Linden.....centre-back...............Holland.........2000/01
Nestor Lorenzo.....................centre-back.................Argentina.......1990/92
Kim Heiselberg.....................left-back.....................Denmark........ 2000
Phillipe Cuervo......................right-midfield...........France........ 1997/2000
Luc Nijholt...........................centre-midfield.........Holland.........1993/95
Ossie Ardiles.........................centre-midfield........Argentina........... 1989
Sofiene Zaaboub....................left-midfield..............France...........2006/08
Jan Age Fjortoft.....................striker.......................Norway.........1993/95
Dave Mitchell........................striker.......................Australia.........1991/93

Subs: Frank Talia, Marko Tuomela, Lilian Nalis, Eric Sabin, Danny Invincibile.

THEY SHALL NOT PASS

Two current Premier League teams have never won at Swindon; Wigan Athletic and Manchester United! Swindon held United to a 2-2 draw in their only ever league meeting in Wiltshire, while a Harold Fleming goal saw them off in 1914 in an FA Cup tie. Scunthorpe United have the worst record at Swindon of current Football League teams, having not won at Swindon in ten attempts. Among the other sides never to win at the County Ground in more than one try are York City (seven attempts), Rochdale (six), Aberdare Athletic (six) and Bradford Park Avenue (four).

LEAGUE CUP TREBLES

The following Swindon players have bagged League Cup hat-tricks, with Jimmy Quinn scoring in consecutive rounds.

Jack Smith ....Swindon v Darlington 1962......................4-0
Peter Noble.....................Swansea v Swindon 1969..........................3-1
Jimmy Quinn ....Swindon v Bristol City 1987....................3-0
Jimmy Quinn ....Swindon v Portsmouth 1987....................3-1
Jan Age Fjortoft ....Charlton v Swindon 1994..........................4-1

THREE GOALS FOR FOREST, THREE POINTS FOR SWINDON

In January 2008 Nottingham Forest visited the County Ground for a League One encounter. Forest managed to score three times and come out on the wrong end of a 2-1 defeat, having put two of those goals into their own net! Firstly, James Perch gave Swindon the lead when he inadvertently turned in Jon-Paul McGovern's free kick . After Forest had equalised, McGovern did the trick again, as Reds defender Ian Breckin headed in the Scotsman's cross to give Swindon a 2-1 win.

DRAWN IN

In 1992, Swindon went through more than a calendar month's worth of draws. The sequence began at Prenton Park on November 22nd in a 0-0 stalemate with Tranmere Rovers. There was then a 1-1 draw with Grimsby Town, a comeback from 2-0 down at Ayresome Park against Middlesbrough, a 0-0 with Ipswich Town, and 1-1 game at Ashton Gate in a Boxing Day derby with Bristol City. It then finished 1-1 at Oakwell against Barnsley. Finally, on New Year's Day 1993, Glenn Hoddle's side cracked the habit, when Millwall were beaten 3-1. Swindon weren't going to let a 3-0 lead slip.

CROFTERS NOT COMFORTABLE

Swindon's home before the move to the County Ground site in the 1890s was The Croft. It wasn't full of luxury facilities – the players had to change at a nearby inn before heading down to the actual pitch.

DERBY DAY HEROES

Eleven Swindon players have scored a hat-trick or better in a local derby with Bristol City, Bristol Rovers, Oxford United or Reading. Harold Fleming leads the way with three hat-tricks, two against Reading and one against Rovers. Freddy Wheatcroft got four goals in one game and three in another while facing the Royals. Tom Wells was the other player to score three against Town's oldest rivals. Jimmy Quinn, Bronco Layne and Frank Peters all got hat-tricks against Bristol City, while Kevin Horlock, Harry Morris and Jack Burkinshaw managed the feat against the Gas. Dave Moss and Arthur Horsfield are the two Town players to put three past an Oxford keeper.

WORTH THE EFFORT

Swindon's effort to lure England schoolboys striker Paul Rideout to the County Ground was well rewarded. As a Hampshire and Southampton schools player, The Dell seemed his logical destination but with his mother coming from Swindon, and Rideout unhappy with his treatment, he ended up at the County Ground where he broke into the first team aged just 16. The club looked after Rideout and his parents well – they helped make him feel settled as they got a job running the club's hostel. Rideout's performances in a struggling Division Four side soon attracted the attention of top flight clubs, including Liverpool, before he was sold to Aston Villa for £250,000. He returned to the County Ground for a loan spell in 1991 in the middle of a globetrotting career that took in Italy, the USA and China, plus scoring the winning goal in the 1995 FA Cup final for Everton.

HARD ACT TO FOLLOW

Shaun Taylor was a brave defender, who would usually appear with lumps on his head from flying boots and all manner of scrapes. You could tell that by the fact he wore a gumshield for matches. He was also a tremendous threat from corners and free kicks. He played more than 250 games for the club, winning the Player of the Season award and helping Town into the top flight. So when Swindon signed his brother Craig, who played for Dorchester Town, you sense he might have an impossible task to match his sibling. Alas that proved to be the case though Taylor mark two was not the worst player by a long way to pull on a Town shirt. He played 59 games in three seasons after being signed by Steve McMahon and scored twice; his long range effort against Queens Park Rangers was something special. He was sold to Plymouth Argyle by Jimmy Quinn.

NUMBER CRUNCHING

At the end of 2008/9, 817 players had played for Swindon Town in Football League matches. Those hitting the landmark numbers of 100 to 800 didn't make a lasting impression, although Ben Tozer did bring in valuable income when the young defender was sold to Newcastle United. For the record Tozer was 800, Wayne Carlisle 700, Austin Berkley 600, Mark Stevens 500, John Bailey 400, Roy Agar 300, Foster Hedley 200 and George Guyan 100.

WE'RE DONE FOR, SO DANCE

In April 1995 Swindon travelled to Sunderland in a game that was key to both sides' chances of survival. The conditions at Roker Park were vile, with torrential rain and a gale lashing the Swindon fans on the terracing. Martin Smith scored the only goal of the game and with a Fjortoft-free side on course for consecutive relegations, there was apparently only one logical response from a drenched travelling support – to launch into an impromptu conga. Swindon's drop into the third tier was confirmed the next week.

Division One Final Table

	P	W	D	L	GF	GA	PTS
20. Sunderland	46	12	18	16	41	45	54
21. Swindon Town (R)	**46**	**12**	**12**	**22**	**54**	**73**	**48**
22. Burnley (R)	**46**	**11**	**13**	**22**	**49**	**74**	**46**
23. Bristol City (R)	**46**	**11**	**12**	**23**	**42**	**63**	**45**
24. Notts County (R)	**46**	**9**	**13**	**24**	**45**	**66**	**40**

CUP FIRSTS

Swindon have never lost in their first matches in a cup competition:

FA Cup
October 23rd 1886 ....Watford Swifts (A) 1-0
Southern Charity Cup
September 22nd 1909.........Bristol Rovers (H)................................4-1
War League Cup
April 13th 1940...................Torquay United (H)..............................1-1
Division Three South Cup
January 12th 1946 ....Bristol City (H)....................................1-1
League Cup
October 12th 1961...............Shrewsbury Town (H)..........................2-2
Anglo Italian Cup
May 2nd 1970.....................Juventus (H) 4-0
Associate Members Cup
February 22nd 1983............Oxford United (A)................................3-1
Full Members Cup
November 10th 1987..........Blackburn Rovers (A) 2-1

MANAGEMENT MATERIAL?

The following Swindon players from 1980 and beyond went on to become Football League managers. It's a list both varied in quality of player and quality of manager. Eddie Howe is obviously a marginal case, as although he spent time at Swindon on loan, he never played for the first team. Colin Calderwood has won promotion with both his clubs, while Martin Ling took Leyton Orient up and sent Oxford United down to the delight of most Swindon fans in 2006. Chic Bates was an assistant manager at Swindon once his playing days had finished. All three of the former Town players who went on to manage the club, coincidentally, were in charge during relegation seasons.

Chic Bates ....Shrewsbury Town & Stoke City
Colin Calderwood......................Northampton Town & Nottingham Forest
Chris Casper .... Bury
Terry Fenwick...Portsmouth & Northampton
Bryan Hamilton .... Tranmere R, Wigan Ath, Leicester C, Norwich C
Eddie Howe...AFC Bournemouth
Paul Ince ....Macclesfield Town, MK Dons, Blackburn Rovers
Chris Kamara...Bradford City & Stoke City
Martin Ling .... Leyton Orient
Dave Moss...Macclesfield
Ray McHale...Scarborough
Iffy Onuora...Swindon
Kieran O'Regan...Halifax Town
Jimmy Quinn.........Reading, Swindon, Shrewsbury & AFC Bournemouth
Lawrie Sanchez... Wycombe Wanderers & Fulham
John Trollope..Swindon
Paul Trollope .... Bristol Rovers
Gary Waddock ....Aldershot Town

THE FLING WITH THE TOP FLIGHT – 1993/94

Swindon's one season in the Premier League saw some famous moments, catastrophic defeats and a string of famous names arrive at the County Ground. They mostly tended to be famous names from 1983 though. The side that won promotion was broken up over the summer, with the departures of Glenn Hoddle, Colin Calderwood and Dave Mitchell, while John Gorman was asked to be manager. An early 5-0 defeat by Liverpool was worrying, but a 5-1 loss at Southampton indicated the problems that would lie ahead. Striker Jan Age Fjortoft just could not score after his big money move from Rapid Vienna. Forwards Andy Mutch and Keith Scott were both signed and it took fourteen games for the first win to arrive, against Queens Park Rangers after Swindon spent most of the match playing with ten men. Scott was on the score-sheet at Liverpool where Swindon had twice taken the lead and were four minutes from winning until Fraser Digby couldn't keep out Mark Wright's header from a corner. Digby's shoulder dislocation at Sheffield Wednesday arguably cost Swindon another win after Gordon Watson scored with Digby lying motionless and the referee unwilling to stop the game. January and February brought hope. Fjortoft started to score and there were wins over Spurs and Coventry City, with the Norwegian getting a hat-trick, before a defeat at Manchester City proved to be the turning point. Swindon were 1-0 up and had an apparently good second disallowed before losing 2-1. An awful 7-1 beating at Newcastle United was followed up by the visit of champions Manchester United. On a heady afternoon, Swindon went behind early. "And that's number one," said Clive Tyldesley on his commentary as Roy Keane scored, anticipating a rout. What he wasn't expecting was an equaliser from Luc Nijholt, Eric Cantona to stamp on John Moncur and get sent off, or Fjortoft's scrambled goal later that gave Swindon a 2-2 draw. By this time several old heads had been brought in, notably Terry Fenwick, Frank McAvennie, Lawrie Sanchez and Brian Kilcline. Relegation was confirmed in a defeat by Wimbledon, but there was one final hurrah. After 20 away games without a win, Swindon got the elusive victory on the road they wanted, at QPR. The reverse side was the final home fixture, a 5-0 crushing by Leeds United. It was a team that could be attractive and flowing but also defensively naive and ruthlessly exposed. But, at least, after 1990, it was there.

Premier League Final Table

	P	W	D	L	GF	GA	PTS
21. Ipswich Town	42	9	16	17	35	58	43
22. Sheffield United (R)	**42**	**8**	**18**	**16**	**42**	**60**	**42**
23. Oldham Athletic (R)	**42**	**9**	**13**	**20**	**42**	**68**	**40**
24. Swindon Town (R)	**42**	**5**	**15**	**22**	**47**	**100**	**30**